INCREDIBLY EASY PROJECT MANAGEMENT

All the things you already know but don't always do

A mildly heretical perspective

Norman Willoughby

2000

Copyright © Norman Willoughby 2000, 2003

All rights reserved. No part of this publication may be reproduced, stored in a retrieval system, or transmitted in any form or by any means, electronic, mechanical, photocopying, recording, or otherwise without the prior permission of the publishers.

First published in Canada by Trafford Publishing to whom thanks are due for permission to publish in the UK

This edition published in 2003 by Management Books 2000 Ltd
Forge House, Limes Road
Kemble, Cirencester
Gloucestershire, GL7 6AD, UK
Tel: 0044 (0) 1285 771441/2
Fax: 0044 (0) 1285 771055
Email: m.b.2000@virgin.net
Web: mb2000.com

Printed and bound in Great Britain by Biddles, Guildford

British Library Cataloguing in Publication Data is available
ISBN 1-85252-434-0

Thank you

**to all those people who, mostly unwittingly,
contributed material to this book**

INCREDIBLY EASY PROJECT MANAGEMENT

An incident that occurred some years ago inspired the title for this Book. I was conducting a structural evaluation and advising an organisation on various aspects of project management. In discussion with one of the younger project managers, she, rather despairingly, said 'Why do you keep saying how easy it is, I like to think that I am doing something difficult!'

A tip of the hat to humility

'They who set themselves to give precepts must of course regard themselves as possessed of greater skill than those to whom they prescribe; and if they err in the slightest particular they subject themselves to censure. But as this tract is put forth merely as a history, or, if you will, as a tale, in which, amid some examples worthy of imitation, there will be found, perhaps, as many more which it were not advisable to follow, I hope it will prove useful to some without being hurtful to any, and that my openness will find some favour with all.'

René Descartes – *A Discourse on Method*

When the Project Manager is besieged on all sides and there seems no way out, remember that things could be worse ... a lot worse. Reflect on the quotation below and try to be equally cheerful under circumstances that, in your darkest hour, may seem painfully similar.

'I went out to Charing Cross, to see Major-general Harrison hanged, drawn and quartered; which was done there, he looking as cheerful as any man could do in that condition.'

Samuel Pepys, October 6, 1660

From *Frederick The Great* by Robert B Asprey, quoting Frederick

'Although he should carefully think out plans beforehand, once in battle he must act decisively: 'It is better to make a bad decision and execute it on the spot than to make no decision.''

5

CONTENTS

6

Contents

Note

This symbol is shown wherever a useful cross-reference is made. The <u>underlined</u> word is the relevant chapter, the other words the appropriate sections to which to refer.

A preamble ...

The Human Side of Management

Project management as a technique is hesitantly being adopted by some segments of almost every business, government, organisation, association. Not too surprising given that the concept can be applied to almost everything we do – from getting up in the morning to going to bed at night. Unfortunately, it is generally easier to appreciate the philosophy than it is to adopt the practice

Managing as a project manager is not greatly different from line management but there are some special pressures that heighten the importance of the project manager's attitude. Scott Adams, creator of Dilbert, perhaps describes it best. He says, 'The project manager's job – trying to get people to get work done when they want to be doing something else and you don't have any authority at all – is a ridiculous position to be in.'

If this is true – no cooperation and no authority – and I assure the reader that Scott Adams is uncomfortably close to the truth – then the project manager's (PM) interaction with others in the enterprise is obviously going to be a major factor in the success or failure of the manager and of the project itself.

Knowing the management techniques is not enough. In both functional management and project management, individual personal motivation should be given far greater consideration in respect of its influence on decision-making than is usual. Personal motivations are especially important when considering proposed improvements to business operations. As an example let us consider the subtle influence of the human factor in the drive to achieve Total Quality Management (TQM) – the equivalent, in my understanding, of the principles of project management.

Writing in the Journal of the Association of Building Engineers, Dr. Paul Watson, PhD MBA MSc MBEng MCIOB MASI Cert Ed, of Sheffield Hallam University in the UK, cites the depressing statistic that 'two out of three organisations engaged in the TQM implementation process considered it a failure'. This high rate of failure may lead one to despair of ever achieving the practical goal of truly cost-effective programme or project execution. But he unerringly puts his finger on the principal deficiencies. In the order in which he gives them, the principal ones are:

- insufficient commitment by senior management
- incorrect corporate culture *(absence of trust and a desire for improvement)*
- no formal implementation strategy
- lack of effective communication
- narrowly based training

Dr. Watson presents a convincing and practical formula for achievement of the innovative goal – the introduction of TQM (I'll use the term TQM in this preamble) – but its application or imposition faces an uphill battle against the frailties of humanity especially that special requirement,'individual personal motivation'.

By the nature of the organisational and resource requirements essential to the successful application of TQM, companies that could benefit most are invariably substantial in financial and human resource assets (a lot of money and a lot of people). They are well-established with a typical functional, hierarchical structure (a bureaucracy). Herein lies the major problem with the acceptance of TQM, by that or any other name and, by extension, of any other management improvement methodology.

Innovative ideas and good intentions, even when – and perhaps especially when – initiated from the top must fight their way through a plethora of covert and overt special-interests within the organisation. *'Yes Minister'*, the BBC television series, was not a comedy of mismanagement so much as a tragedy of self-interests.

Sir Humphrey Appleby, the consummate functionary, showed that, no matter the impetus from the top, no matter the brilliance of the idea, no matter the provable cost-saving, it were well-nigh impossible to change the system if it were not to the immediate, tangible advantage of the individual bureaucrat, manager, functionary, worker at any level, who was required to make the change or adjust to the change. Public companies suffer to a lesser or greater degree from the same syndrome depending largely on that element cited by Dr. Watson – the corporate culture. The bigger the company, the more worthwhile is TQM. Correspondingly, the greater are the prejudices and the instinctive, as well as the artificially-created, road-blocks to be overcome.

It may be unfair to impute malicious contrariness to those who perceive a threat to their status, their influence or their financial well-being. As often as not it is a simple but powerful *unconscious* reluctance to change; a similarly *unconscious* refusal to recognise the potential benefit to the whole rather than the disadvantage to the part. Often as not the immovable object can justify its objections by means either of an inner or external well-rationalised objection.

The disparate operations of large enterprises tend, by the nature of the beast, to remain hidden in their detail both from upper management and other functional management streams. This is usually a source of comfort and security to the departmental denizens and leads them to consider as more important what they are convinced they are doing well in contrast to the other departments that are constantly impeding their effectiveness.

The higher in the organisation, likely the older the functionary and so the more deep-seated the resistance to innovation. We are constrained to accept their justifications of the status quo because, though we know that human beings are essentially egocentric, there is a reluctance to impute it, even obliquely, to others for fear of identifying it in ourselves. But in fact we are all (except the perceptive readers of this book) driven by 'don't encroach on my turf; don't threaten my salary, my pension, my perks or my prejudices'; above all, 'don't diminish my authority'.

These, I fear, are the controlling factors in the success or failure of TQM or of any other innovation in management. The essential commitment to improvement, to change by senior management must continue beyond the initiation of the restructuring process. As Dr. Watson suggests, it is not enough to set the process in train and then simply leave it to the experts. Senior management must keep in mind the inherent emotional and psychological factors of resistance and be meticulous in its monitoring of the process of change and absolutely ruthless in its pursuit of the goal. If this is made clear from the outset and, if perceived or suspected reluctance to adopt new methodologies incurs immediate sanction from the top, the possibility of success is enormously enhanced. In fact success rises to the level of probability.

Who should analyse and recommend?

I suggest that the employment of external consultants for strategic analysis is an essential of the process. Even the largest organisations cannot find staff so remote from the personnel involved or so personally disinterested in operations that they can be completely impartial in determining the requirements for improvement. Needful to say, the selection of the appropriate consultants is as important as first determining to undertake the strategic analysis that will generate change. In this regard bigger is not necessarily better and a proven track record by an expanding consultant company may ultimately fail of its own momentum of growth; better this happen to a company other than yours.

Detailed, incontrovertible terms of reference (TOR) for the consultant with as many checks, balances and guarantees as the candidate can be induced to accept are essential. Beyond that, without interfering unnecessarily, it is essential constantly to monitor the consultant's procedures. The monitor, preferably an insider known (or at least, believed) to have the true interests of the employer at heart, to the extent even of welcoming innovation, must be accoutred with an insatiable curiosity, a well-developed disregard for other people's opinion of his or her personality and a reputation for nit-picking. This will enable the monitor to evaluate the nit-picking capacity of the approved consultant.

In my own experience as a consultant, consensus within an organisation was most readily achieved in those cases where the re-structuring was a pre-condition of future external financing; perhaps not surprising – the carrot and the stick. In a specific instance where the conditions were theoretically ideal, the proposed re-organisation of a substantial enterprise (a luxury property developer in the Algarve, Portugal), was sabotaged by its own sales department when it was proposed that it (the Sales Department) concede design and engineering control to the architecture and engineering department. Incredible perhaps and laughable had it not been for the insolvency that was the eventual result of this intransigence.

Such companies, too frequently on the verge of collapse from poor management practices, even when receptive to change, often do not have the resources or cash-flow to see the process through to completion with sufficient subsequent time to reap the benefits; perhaps one reason for the high failure rate of TQM. However, for a structure that does not absolutely depend for its survival on management improvements (government departments, for instance) the exercise is salutary and most probably will generate unexpected benefits in the future when all the fuss and furore have died down and the initiators (instigators?) have been promoted or transferred out of harms way and are no longer a threat to the moral authority of the subjects or sufferers of change. Large companies, financially-viable but seeking efficiencies, have the best chance of success and should certainly give it a try. Tightly-integrated professionals with a common corporate objective could undoubtedly benefit from the introduction of TQM without serious disruption to their activities.

However, despite the importance of the authority of upper management in fostering innovation, its absence need not cause lowly-placed innovators to despair completely. Every member of every organisation, if sufficiently yet circumspectly inspired by a desire for improvement, can start the process by subtly introducing small remedies at his or her level of activity. Indeed, it is arguable that this is a contracted obligation of every employee – an inherent duty to the shareholders or the taxpayer.

A rigorous application, and sensitive re-moulding where necessary, of useful procedures that already exist but which are usually ignored can begin the process. If there are sufficient interested staff willing to stick their necks out just a little way, together or independently of each other, substantial improvement can be achieved over time. Slow, yes; but, if one is willing to work unheralded then PQM (Partial Quality Management!) in the example above may be a beneficial first step on the road to Total Quality Management.

Please do not attribute to me an unjustified cynicism. Look around at your own organisation and consider whether it can stand some organisational improvement and how difficult it would be to introduce TQM changes.

Having said all that; having suggested that introducing TQM or project management might be beyond normal human skills, I should point to the other side of the coin. According to Dr. Watson's statistic, one out of three actually consider TQM a success. If you decide to embark on the adventure – and you should if you are in any way project-oriented – then this book will tell you how to overcome the problems that you can be sure you will face.

Introduction

Project management in 2003 AD is not materially different from 2003 BC. Building the pyramids was no easier than a modern hydro-electric project. Be sure that the Pharaoh's project manager had the same organisational and personality problems with his staff and his client as we do today. The philosophical aspects have not changed one iota and are logical and uncomplicated. They can be learned from a book, through journals or in school. What is more difficult to teach and even more difficult to absorb are those aspects of the character of a project manager that are the motivating force that creates the conditions for a successful project.

It takes certain unusual personality traits and workplace experiences to confront and overcome the problems inevitably encountered in a project management environment. They are usually found where least expected and at every level, in every situation.

The project manager's perspective must be such that it leads logically and inevitably to the right solutions. This will be dictated, in each case, by that essential, basic core philosophy of the project manager, the desire to do a good job. That philosophy should be expressed as ...

**'This is my project and I shall do every proper thing
to make it succeed'.**

Technology, training and experience are important. Nevertheless, good project management first requires common-sense, patience, discretion, self-discipline, the proper **attitude** ... and perhaps a thick skin.

Some of this book's topics may seem simplistic. But remember the subtitle; *'all the things you already know but don't always do'*. If I am reminding you of something you already know while revealing its true importance, then I have succeeded. Every project manager can benefit from constant self-reminders that these are basic premises that are known, too often ignored but **must** be followed if success is to be achieved. The presentation is in more or less alphabetical order under a few main section headings. Some subjects are included under several sections in varying detail but there are ample cross-references. Anecdotes (maybe more frightening than amusing) to illustrate the text are enclosed in boxes and salutary exhortations and warnings are scattered throughout, also in boxes.

This Second (UK) Edition enlarges on several of the subjects, allows for a readership much wider than originally anticipated and contains more illustrative anecdotes.

This edition has more illustrative accounts, especially in respect of monitoring, and additional material to keep pace with the practical issues created by new technology. Do you, too, have difficulty keeping up with communication advances? But the basic principles of good management in this regard do not change. Make sure that information is properly conveyed; make sure it has been completely received and check, double-check and check again.

So take what you find useful from the guidelines in this book and above all, concentrate on your attitude and you will have discovered ...

INCREDIBLY EASY PROJECT MANAGEMENT

1

Planning

Good planning is the foundation stone of good implementation

General

Is it too obvious to say that planning is the stage at which a project may be, and very often is, most easily ruined? Good planning is the foundation stone of good implementation. Planning and implementation should never be divorced from each other. Simply put, if the planner ceases to be responsible at the project approval stage, s/he may, justifiably or not, disclaim any responsibility when things go wrong during implementation.

Conversely, a planner who anticipates remaining on the team throughout implementation will certainly find earnest motivation in the potential for disapprobation of his or her colleagues should the planning prove faulty. *Put a little less subtly; the team will make her or his life hell if s/he has fouled up the planning!*

The project manager should be fully engaged and informed (preferably 'in charge' – in control) through the planning stage and carry full responsibility through the life of the project.

Both planning and implementation should be under the full control of the project manager

The key to successful planning, whether the project be large or small, is logical thought process. Because the thoughts must be successfully communicated, it is easier to channel the process through commonly accepted methodologies and terminologies.

- **Goal** is generally accepted as a broad, strategic objective into which a project fits.
- **Purpose** is the primary end objective of the project.
- **Output(s)** is the product resulting from the implementation of the project.
- **Input(s)** is the requirement of service, finance and materiel that will produce the output.

There is another measure of achievement, 'Results', briefly mentioned later in this section and in Appendix A. 'Results' as criteria of success have been around a long time but their interpretation and measurement is disputatious and would neither affect nor clarify what follows.

Goal

Although the logic of project development places 'goal' first as an objective, it will only be briefly mentioned here. Except in large projects or in respect of 'programmes' (a series or bunch of related projects), it has a limited importance in the context used in this book. Others sometimes define goal as sole objective. Nevertheless, it should be considered. It is a question of putting the project into the context of the larger order of development.

For instance, a project that seeks to improve prenatal health care in a village of a few hundred people may have as a goal 'to contribute to the overall improvement of health conditions in 'X' country'. While this is true and important, the wider context is probably not significant in terms of the primary success of the proposed project – though it may need to be stated formally, in that it may contribute to a larger **programme** of varied projects.

It is equally important, for instance, for a property developer or an engineering company and their staff to be aware of goal. This is often not the case; there is an awareness that the enterprise should expand and make money but, often, management will not have stated in clear terms either the context of the current project or the overall objective to be achieved. Looking at any project from the perspective of 'goal' can often reveal inadequacies not perceived when viewed in the short term and the more limited context of 'purpose'. This applies equally, for instance, to a small contractor as to a large government department. Decide the context in which you are working. What is your ultimate objective (goal) and will your projects help to achieve it?

📖 '*Communication, Language, Definitions*'

Purpose

The above-mentioned fundamentals of order in both planning and implementation should not, indeed cannot, properly be avoided. A well-expressed purpose becomes the key to all activities that are in doubt. Asking the question 'does it lead to achievement of the purpose?' assists in resolving many problems.

The purpose of a typical construction project, for instance, is not just the creation of an apartment building (that is an output) – more likely, it is to provide an income from rental revenue or to produce a capital gain. Purpose of a health project may be a decrease in infant mortality. The output (the primary physical manifestation of the project) could be considered as a new clinic or maybe an education programme.

Output

Similarly, tabulating outputs, helps in rationalising both the methodology of implementation and the financial and material resources required (the inputs) to provide the outputs. It is not always easy to state inputs and outputs in simple terms; a guideline is to try to use terms that have a basis in measurement. In such projects as a construction exercise or material supply, the output is more easily recognised (eg: a house at a value of £250,000 or 2,000 tons of fertiliser).

An output in a computer software environment might be stated as '1.5 million copies of a broad-based spreadsheet to retail at £130 over a period of 10 months' – a physical, measurable commodity.

Outputs for management improvement projects, for instance, or for an overseas aid project are not so simple nor so obvious but to illustrate, for an aid project, an output vaguely stated as 'increase in production of corn' would be better expressed in terms of the percentage improvement in quantity over an existing known quantity (while maintaining an equal quality) or of the anticipated quantity of the crop by weight or volume on completion of the project. Failure so to quantify or value the output will make project monitoring and evaluation impossible.

Input

Inputs usually have an element of finance that is obviously measurable. Other inputs such as labour and services included in management activities should be calculated on a time basis and valued accordingly. For instance, an input could be 40 hours of project management time which would carry an appropriate value in either local (foreign site) or national terms depending on who is providing the service.

The order of thought is important. Analyse the purpose very clearly and determine its nature with certainty before contemplating either outputs or inputs. Next, decide what outputs will achieve the purpose and finally, the inputs that would lead to the outputs. A purpose is often limited or determined by the funds available – usually a known factor. It certainly should be a known factor.

This may seem a simple and obvious approach ... and it is. It is the consideration of the many things that may go wrong that starts to complicate the planning of the project. In the 'sophisticated' western world, the smooth running of a project cannot be guaranteed; overseas, either in the developed or in the developing world, there are many more unknowns and even more care is required.

Nevertheless, as many potential limitations to success as possible must be taken into account in the planning and some time must be allowed for approvals, deliveries, bad weather, failures to communicate, monitoring, remedial activities, accidents, cultural differences, work ethics and so on. An unrealistic approach to project planning will only lead to multiple problems during implementation. In this respect, a tendency towards pessimism is advantageous.

In respect of each level (purpose, outputs, inputs) take into account as many hazards as can rationally be imagined and adjust the inputs and outputs accordingly. The purpose should not be changed unless it clearly cannot be achieved. In such a circumstance (that of a revised purpose), a new project is required with all new outputs and inputs. It is better to change the project (decide on a more realistic purpose) and risk a delay than it is to try to force the inputs and outputs to fit the original purpose.

Strictly speaking and perhaps comfortingly, it doesn't matter what you call all these things: what you are looking for, within an overall context (goal), is the reason for the project (purpose), the tangible results you expect (outputs) and what you first need to make it all possible (inputs). Incredibly easy!

📖 *'Planning, Logical Framework Analysis'* and *'Appendix, LFA'*

Attitude

As in all aspects of project management, perhaps the most important consideration in planning and management of a project is 'attitude' – the 'attitude' of the project manager and the team. The project must be approached in a professional manner. A small project requires as equal a consideration of all significant factors as does a large one. The quantity of information required for a small project may be less but all the elements of a good project plan must be there. Do not neglect to pay attention to the principles of the essential steps because the project costs less or has a lower profile than others on your agenda. Certainly, you will not spend as much time on a small project (though, as a percentage, your input will actually be greater) but you must maintain the same professional perspective.

Another aspect of the attitude of professionalism is the importance of the project manager maintaining a personal disinterestedness in respect of the technical content of the project. Unless you are a one-man team (which is not unknown), it is important not to second-guess your team experts. You may sometimes know the technical aspects of the project as well as or better than your team member but the required technique is to draw the information out of your expert, guiding him or her along the lines that you think are correct without building up a counter-productive antagonism. The expert's record of success and your common sense will guide you in determining what questions to ask and what recommendations to accept.

Learn to be patient no matter how difficult or painful it may be under these special circumstances. Nevertheless, if the member is clearly on the wrong track, giving doubtful advice and is recalcitrant when chided, you may have to dispense with his or her services. Not a major problem in the case of a consultant team member but seriously fraught with ill consequences in a matrix environment of a single organisation.

 *'Organisation, Confrontation'*

Approvals

General
Without denying the indispensability of approvals to the acceptable completion of a project, they are one of the least-considered, potential **impediments** to effective planning and scheduling. In a bureaucracy or long-established hierarchy especially, approvals may eat up more planning time than the planning exercise itself (it may happen during implementation,

too). One may as well be realistic at the start of planning. Show the approval process as it **truly** is, indicating each person or position that has the opportunity to stop or delay the process. Assign a **realistic** time to each 'review' or approval. Err on the side of pessimism – most projects give more cause for pessimism than for optimism.

If the approval authorities are sceptical and accuse the planner or project manager (as project scheduler) of exaggerating potential delays in order to create additional lead-time, ask them to offer shorter review and approval times based on their own view of their timetable and capacity for making decisions (better not state it in those terms!). They will usually be optimistic – which gives the project manager a club with which to harass the hierarchy should it begin to display the customary indications of falling behind on approvals. Make sure they abide by their agreed, established times.

An approval may be as simple as passing a project plan to the immediate superior for a review prior to forwarding it to a committee. This is an approval, whatever name it be given and it should be included in the 'approval schedule'. I have seen documents sit for days on a middle-level manager's desk while he or she dealt with the other snapping alligators first. This is quite understandable from their point of view but does nothing to advance the project and must be anticipated and thwarted by the project manager.

My own technique for ensuring prompt approvals is to obtain the early cooperation of the top authorising officer by judicious cajoling while stimulating the upper echelon's own optimism – in the very early stages of the project and before it has become obvious what a nuisance I am going to be. Then camp outside his or her office every time an approval is needed until it is provided. He or she may loathe you at the time but, when the project meets the schedule, the importuning will be forgotten (or, at least, relegated to the back of the mind until the next project is scheduled). If you survive the first project, you may find that your irritant factor persuades the bosses to give prompt approvals the next time to get you out of their hair.

Carry the documentation personally from desk to desk, from approval to approval. Put it directly into the hands of your immediate superior if there is a 'review' required. Do not drop it in your out-tray or even the superior's in-tray and hope it will arrive on time or be seen on time. If you feel that this chore is demeaning, that you are entitled to rely on the 'system' – remember that it is your project and your deadline.

Do not let the approving officer or body off the hook. If he, she or they insist on 'tomorrow', say, reluctantly but definitively, 'I will be back at such and such an hour' and obtain agreement to that time – write it ostentatiously in your diary. Make a thorough nuisance of yourself. It gets action. (But, don't be late!) When you return for the approved documents perhaps to find they still lack a signature, hover until it is appended. If you are ejected from the holy precincts, be specific and positive about when you will return. Do not ease the pressure.

This is an effective technique. But being tenacious about approvals is not enough of itself. You must be equally effective in all the other aspects of project management or your 'tenacity' will be discounted as incompatible with your other capacities. This could be the kiss of death to your immediate effectiveness and the harbinger of an untimely end to a career. This is all a question of that same 'attitude' mentioned in the Introduction; you have to be consistent in all your actions. If you are going to be effective, you must be effective all the time and in all endeavours or you will be found out eventually.

A detailed bar chart of project development probably provides the most graphic illustration of the impediment that reviews and approvals impose on the planning process. If you find it necessary to demonstrate the problem (and it often is), prepare a chart similar in concept to that shown in the illustration opposite. Most people will be startled and disbelieving at the very real effect of requirements for multiple approvals, no matter that the approval be informal or formal. Do not depreciate the informal approvals; they have a substantial effect on project progress. The chart can be prepared fairly quickly, without benefit of computer, by anyone with a thorough knowledge of the project and its hierarchical context. If you already have the project in a computer schedule, it should be even more effective as an illustration – everybody believes a computer.

Boards of Directors and committees require more care in handling. A board (with powers of approval) usually meets periodically; not all members are instantly available. Should your plan or proposal miss a meeting, you may have to wait a month for the next session or be required to beg for an extraordinary meeting. So, if you miss a scheduled approval, you undermine your credibility. Always make sure that if there are any delays in approvals, they are caused by the approval authority – not the project team and, especially, not by the project manager.

A construction contractor working for a single client has the same problems on a different scale. When agreeing the contract, establish a schedule of approvals for the client and attach it as an annex of the contract. Make sure the client knows that tile colours, floor coverings, hardware, bathroom fixtures and so on have to be selected at specified times and that a limited time is available to do so. However, make sure that you provide all the information at the right time and that approvals are recorded (initials on a dated sample, for example).

PROJECT DEVELOPMENT AND APPROVAL SCHEDULE

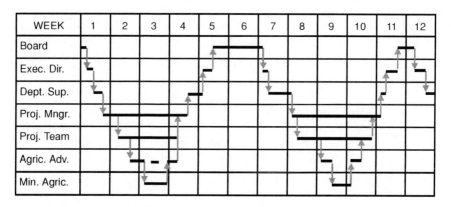

In this example, about 50% is productive time and 50% is review and approve. Unfortunately, this is not an unusual division of project planning time.

The technique of letting others determine an optimistic schedule applies similarly to the scheduling of other elements of the project team. After proper discussion, let the team member or consultant suggest his/her own time-frame. Usually, it will be optimistic. If it is not, if it is unreasonably protracted, be patient and discuss the timing rationally until it approaches the requirements of the schedule. Then try to make sure that the new time-frame is seen as having been volunteered and not imposed.

I prepared a similar chart for an organisation that always assumed two years as a standard project planning estimate. The chart showed that multiple approvals by layers of committees imposed a minimum three-year and more often a four-year planning period. Everyone was astonished; management had become so accustomed to the longer planning period that the target had been forgotten and the longer period accepted in practice while planning procedures manuals still paid lip-service to the target.

Of course, it is no use being so clever in these scheduling techniques that you lose sight of what is feasible. Be sure that you, as project manager, don't set targets that you can't handle.

> **The project manager must remember always: 'I am responsible for the project!' Do not allow the project to be delayed by any other participant**

📖 *'Communication, Charts & Diagrams, ORGANIGRAM, Control'* and *'Responsibility, Approvals'*

Authorities having jurisdiction

A different problem is presented by those approvals required of authorities outside the organisation or otherwise beyond the client's control but which have legal jurisdiction over some aspect of the project.

A government ministry, a municipal authority, a standards organisation or, for overseas projects, any number of bureaucratic entities may have a watching brief and final approval on the implementation of a project. Their attitude towards the project will be governed by their own immediate interest, the rules and regulations governing the project and current 'political' considerations.

There are different methods of influencing government behaviour but this is not a call for lobbying. Given that all matters are being properly conducted, the correct method of ensuring proper consideration of the project at the proper time is to communicate the schedule in as transparent and timely a manner as possible.

Make sure that the nature of the approvals is indicated, that the required approval dates are firm and that a reasonable approval period is allowed.

- Ensure that the information is complete.
- Submit this information as soon as it is available.
- Change it as necessary but no more than that, after the first submission.
- Always forewarn the appropriate department of each approval with sufficient notice to inhibit procrastination.
- Establish the date at which the approved documents will be returned; offer to collect them in person.
- Several days before the approval is due, advise them that you will be there (this can be done, unobjectionably, by making an enquiry as to

the exact location for collection and the name of the person who will hand over the documents).

There are many different levels of approval by authorities having jurisdiction. The above is a recommendation of the **philosophy** of approach; it will serve as a guideline only; adapt it for each special situation. The objective is to persuade the 'authority' to adhere to your timetable and, at the same time, for you to be obviously efficient without giving offence. Don't, in other words, shout your efficiency so loudly that the authority feels morally diminished. There is an inherent negativism in bureaucracy that is all too easily stimulated by perceived contrariness or condescension on the part of the 'public'.

Perhaps you were not aware that effectiveness and efficiency are offensive. Let me assure you that many people find it so – certainly, in others – when either they cannot claim it for themselves or are unaware of its manifestations.

Budget

Getting the budget right at the planning stage is not easy – some might say it is impossible. There are two common approaches to budgeting. First, a feasibility study (formal or otherwise) that recommends a certain expenditure will already have been prepared. This is the base for the development and adjustment of the project budget. Second, there is a fixed sum available within which project elements must be fitted and adjusted.

To some extent the latter is the easier because you have at least one firm criterion for developing the project – assuming that the project is sufficiently flexible to permit either magnitude (scope) or quality to be modified.

Obviously, the client (outside or inside your organisation) will still want as much as possible for the money but a fixed financial limitation in the back (or the front) of everyone's mind may put a damper on the over-enthusiastic team member whose vision may be more expansive than the client's or department's pocket.

Should there already exist a feasibility or similar study with financial recommendations, those recommendations must be tested and justified by the team. This is not only time-consuming but may cause conflict – depending on the origins of the study. Not many people welcome the questioning of their recommendations. Obviously someone high up will have approved or accepted the study so the political and career difficulties and dangers are obvious. (If you must tread on toes, try to do it lightly!)

However, unless the client or superior (your superior is your client, too) is prepared to state categorically that the budget as presented is untouchable, then it must be validated at the earliest possible planning stage.

> *Before the days of the universal computer, I had spent several weeks developing budgets for 12 projects in a large programme. Forty-eight hours before facing the Programme Approval Committee, the programme budget was cut by 10%. I was required to re-calculate 12 multiple-element project budgets (including percentage contingencies and risk factors) to arrive at the new overall total. There are computer-free ways of doing this but I would rather not expose them to scrutiny.*

A client is inclined to look at the final budget figure and not question so closely as the project manager how the figure was calculated. The responsibility for accuracy is that of the project manager. Because cost is usually the most critical item in project development, be absolutely sure of the validity of your figures and those of your advisors or team members.

> *I was fortunate to work with a QS/Building Economist who could estimate a $20 million project based on layout plans of 1/16' scale (architectural & structural), a few cross sections and an outline specification. He was very experienced and had a wealth of data from previous projects but, even so, this was no small achievement. Of course, he had to be able to say as the project proceeded, for example, 'No, you cannot use better quality tiles' or 'No, marble floors are not in the cost plan'. To ignore his recommendations was to jeopardise the budget.*

Calculate every budget item to the **degree of accuracy possible at the time**, based on the increasing availability of information as planning progresses (there is a tendency to say 'we can go into more detail later'- this is not good enough). It is comparatively simple to update with a computer but the activity should not be deferred or neglected simply because it can now be done quickly; do not postpone the incorporation of any budgetary variances until they have developed their own unstoppable momentum – it is incredible how quickly the whole thing can get out of hand. Update the budget now.

For construction projects, it is usual and accepted to have a quantity surveyor (QS), estimator or building economist on the team. Other types of projects will benefit from employing a corresponding cost control expert appropriate to the inputs and outputs of the project. But, I repeat, the responsibility is still that of the project manager (PM); if the budget advisor does a poor job, the PM should and will take the blame.

📖 *'Parameters, Cost'*

Charts and diagrams

The usefulness of charts and diagrams for presentation purposes, for developing relationships, for displaying true project control and for assisting in clarifying thinking are extolled and commended in the section, *'Communication, Charts and Diagrams'*.

The graphic presentation of the Project Development and Approval Schedule under 'Approvals' in this section ('PLANNING'), demonstrates instantly the need to keep approval time and number to a minimum. It would take pages of written material and a great deal of clever talking to convey an effect the equal of the chart.

Some charts and tables that are usefully included in a plan of operation to condense and clarify the information it contains are:l

- Financial Procedures (if not included in the organigram)
- Implementation Schedule
- Logical Framework Analysis
- Monitoring Cost Calculation
- Monitoring Schedule
- Organigram (organisation chart)
- Procurement procedures
- Responsibility/Activity Matrix
- Disbursement Authorities
- Schedule of Approvals
- Work breakdown structure (WBS)

📖 *'Communication, Charts & Diagrams'*

Checking

The best advice my father gave me was to 'check, double-check and check again'. I have not always followed his guidance and when I haven't, I have usually ended up in minor or major trouble.

Checking, review, critique, verification, whatever it be called, is one of the essentials of all stages of good project management but listed here under 'Planning' as being the first step in actual project development. Not only should you check your own work, you should check everyone else's, or make sure that it is checked by someone responsible and always have your own material checked by others wherever possible. This is good for the project manager's psyche; it encourages humility.

As an illustration of the importance of checking and the implications of its absence; a set of construction drawings with spaces for four signatures, as follows ...

1. Designed by:	3. Checked by:
2. Drawn by:	4. Approved by:

might lack the first two without much consequence but should not be accepted if they lack the third and fourth (checked/approved). It is not even safe to assume that the fourth signature without the third will guarantee the **correctness** of the document (here we are discussing accuracy, not responsibility). You will often find documents approved that have not been checked; an example, perhaps, of the desperation under pressure that sometimes attends the irresolute project manager or design manager who has been unwise enough to accept that the schedule is more important than accuracy. (We can fix that later!)

The **third** signature is the important one; it means that someone has been prepared to stick his or her neck out and imparts a validity to the documents that, otherwise, they do not have. If you are an experienced project manager you will not be surprised at how difficult it is to obtain that signature and, indeed, how often no provision is made for checking – because it is onerous, time-consuming and even **frightening**.

Many organisations do not have a standard procedure for checking and it falls to the manager or project manager to persuade (con?) someone into undertaking the task. Any sensible person who is not obligated to check something will instinctively refuse. Some, if pressured, will perform reluctantly and perhaps not to the desired standard. This is more dangerous than not checking because the product (drawings, plans, studies, reports, whatever) will be given a legitimacy it does not merit.

In fact, the '**fear of checking**' is so universal that there is an accepted but unvoiced conspiracy in many hierarchies across many industries to ignore the requirement – it is often in fact not demanded at all (even when it is an official procedural requirement), as it should be ... **always!** It may seem unnecessary to say this but the project manager who insists on this policy should take into account that it will surely prejudice the schedule unless **everyone is totally aware of the requirement when planning begins** and everyone really **believes** that it will be enforced.

An industry acknowledgement of the significance of checking is exemplified by a large, well-known, successful construction company with origins in the U.K. and world-wide operations. It has a special section in the architecture department devoted entirely to checking drawings and specifications; architectural against structural, mechanical against electrical and all against each other. The work is tedious and special allowance is made for extra cups of coffee (or tea) and long periods gazing out the window. The checkers are mostly practical tradesmen who know from experience that it is well to provide for passage of piping from one side of a structural member to the other and that a convector heater should not be stood in front of a floor to ceiling window. How many times have you seen exactly that? The tolerance for apparent laxity in work behaviour in this department illustrates the difficulty experienced in finding willing checkers, the boredom inherent in the work and its importance to project success.

If, well into the project, the project manager suddenly decides that 'from now on, all work must be checked and certified as such', there will be revolution in the ranks. Make sure that this logical, essential requirement is understood and appreciated by everyone engaged on the project from the very first day. The apparent, immediate delays that sometimes result from systematic checking are usually inconsequential, trivial, compared to the delays and extra cost (to either client or project manager), not to mention loss of face, that faulty information can cause. In fact, of course, proper checking, properly scheduled will **eliminate**, or at the very least minimise, delays.

All planning and contract documents (by their nature) do not arrive with a 'checked by' warranty, nor even a method of determining that there has been a 'checking' procedure. If a document is to be used as an important complement of a project and arrives unheralded or without some acceptable affirmation of authenticity and accuracy, either ask for corroboration in writing or write an acknowledgement of receipt that makes it clear how the document will be used and the importance of its accuracy.

*Something such as: 'Thank you for the Pampas Project soil analysis data, received on ...(date). This latest revision (dated ...) will provide the critical, definitive information for the development of the final Plan of Operation from which productivity projections will be determined **and on which the decision to proceed with the project will be based.'*** (The bold-facing is required and makes the purpose clear while giving a warning of its criticality.)

Then, make sure that your letter has been received and understood at the right level of authority, either by mention at a subsequent meeting or by a recorded, follow-up phone call.

📖   *'Communication, Follow-up'*

How firmly you state the situation is a question of the importance of the material. However, do not neglect this sort of recording. It is not just a question of protecting your position (although that is important) but of making sure that all information is communicated in unquestionable terms while trying to avoid the sort of overt brutality that may prejudice a good working relationship. It is not always possible to avoid hurting feelings but the project comes first.

Checking is one of the most important project planning and implementation procedures

---

To return to the example of a set of construction drawings. A project manager or the responsible team member, receiving drawings (that contain spaces labelled 'checked by', 'approved by') should reject them if they contain no initials or signature. In such a case, it is obvious that the designer has accepted and agreed the need for such a confirmation and, in not supplying it, casts into doubt the value of the documents.

If no such requirement is shown on the drawings, you are safe in assuming that the warranty of accuracy is inherent in the submission of the drawings. If you wish to be meticulous to the point of offensiveness, write a receipt indicating that you assume the designs have been thoroughly checked and approved accordingly. Of course, if there is a professional architect's or engineer's signature and stamp, that person is accepting full responsibility for everything contained in the documents. I use drawings as an example; the principle applies to all project material.

I feel more comfortable if I know that someone has checked the documents. The fact that someone else agrees either contractually or simply 'in effect' to be accountable for costs resulting from erroneous drawings or other documents, does not relieve you, the project manager, of all the problems consequent on those errors nor prevent delays in completion of the project.

Contracts

From the first step in planning, it is obvious that there will be a requirement for the development and codification of relationships within and without the project team. It saves time, money and a lot of aggravation to consider **all relationships** as possible scenarios for a formal contract. By doing this you will develop the 'perspective' and the data that can be interpreted in either the context and format of a contract, or as a job description, as elements in an organigram, as parts of an activity matrix, in the description of a project development strategy and so on. Remember that when planning commences the project manager may have only the loosest idea of how the project is to be organised and implemented. Within a large organisation, being able to present a well-thought-out work description and organisational structure to another department places you at a substantial advantage in negotiating your working relationship.

'Perspective' is the significant word in this process. Firm adherence to a formal thought process in a contract context obviates the creation of casual relationships that are founded too much in the anticipation of good faith and not enough in rights and obligations.

Small general construction contractors should particularly note this point. A previously good working relationship with a sub-contractor does not negate the need for a proper contract containing, amongst other things, a comprehensive description of the work required. Companies or government departments that employ consultants on a regular basis may find themselves in a similar situation. Good relationships founder very easily when things go wrong.

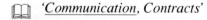 *'Communication, Contracts'*

Control

Reiteration in this book of **'whoever controls the money, controls the project'** may appear unnecessarily heavy-handed but it merits constant repetition. Keep it always in mind but especially during planning. It may be too late to make changes after the plan of operation (POP) has been approved. Although POPs by their nature may be modified, casually-entrenched authority is incredibly difficult to revoke – it will be strenuously resisted by those who have acquired it. If authority over disbursement is inadvertently or by undue influence put in the wrong hands, wresting it from their grasp will be infinitely more difficult than making sure it was in the right hands in the first place.

Too often, these things are not noticed during the planning of a complex project. An unintentional qualification to a relationship slips in and has a contractual, legal or control significance during implementation that was neither intended nor anticipated. Check every relationship against this significant criterion: **'who controls the money?'**

For instance, a contract that is nominally under the control of the project manager but for which payments are indicated as being approved by another is effectively under the control of the other. Of course, this may be a perfectly proper activity and authority but make sure that is what you intend.. After all, we are all on the same side and there is no reason to assume that approval will be withheld. However, that is not the salient point. Keep as much as possible of the control where it belongs – in the hands of the project manager. But don't get carried away by the exuberance of power; it is still the 'client' who must be served and the client who foots the bill or represents those that foot the bill. If you are in government, remember well that the ultimate 'client' is the taxpayer.

Money control = project control

The organigram (organisation chart) should show the lines of control of the project. If the lines do not clearly indicate the flow of control parallelling the flow of money, then either there is an error in the organigram or in the planning concept. Preparing the organigram in the first stages of planning (and modifying it as you proceed) will enable you to perceive any anomalies that could prejudice the smooth running of the project.

📖 *'Communication, Charts & Diagrams, Organigram'*; *'Responsibility, Control'* and *'Organisation, Control'*

Logical framework analysis

One of the most useful aids to project planning is the Logical Framework

Analysis Chart (LFA) or the Logical Framework Approach. It organises the analytical thought process in such a way that, when the chart is properly completed, no room is left for doubt that the inputs will produce the objectives.

This is not to suggest that the analysis chart is easy to use or even that it is the complete answer to all your planning needs. Two people, independently developing the LFA from the same information data base for the same project may easily arrive at different conclusions – but only because one or both have made a misinterpretation in the process. *This may lead to a lot of friendly debate or fierce argument – but invariably helps in the planning of the project.*

The LFA is an extremely valuable tool and provides a framework for discussion and rationalisation as well as for logic. Just don't expect it to bring revelation to the project development process in a blinding flash. Keep at it till you get it right and do not prepare it in isolation. Make sure that it is freely discussed and do not hesitate to obtain disinterested opinions from helpful colleagues; that is, from outside the team or even the department.

Every project manager is advised to become familiar with the LFA; use it as the basic planning tool as well as for feasibility analysis and as a mainstay of project evaluation.

📖 *'Communication, Charts & Diagrams'* and *'Appendix, LFA'*

Monitoring

Monitoring is rarely accorded its proper importance either in planning as a required, indeed essential, activity, or in budgeting, as an expenditure item. It is essential to have an adequate budget for this activity. Inadequate monitoring or inspection due to poor budget preparation, as well as deficient reporting for time, cost and quality will quickly destroy the most cleverly designed cost control and scheduling system and the project with them.

Monitoring should always be considered a continuing exercise; not something intermittent. There are different levels in the detail of monitoring but, should the plan of operation not include financial and activity provisions for some sort of overview as a continuous operation, then there is something wrong with the plan. A complete section of the book is devoted to this supremely important activity.

📖 *'Monitoring'* chapter

Plan of operation

A plan of operation (POP) should be designed to answer all the questions that might arise during the planning, implementation and evaluation of a project.

The amount of information and the magnitude of detail it contains is always dependent on the peculiarities of the project. No two projects are ever identical, so similar POPs are the exception rather than the rule. The similarities that exist lie in the fact that each POP requires specific responses to comparable questions; the detail contained in the response is the variable.

For instance, a POP that includes operations of an 'executing agency' would contain the usual 'Responsibilities' and 'Roles' sections but would require very exhaustive detail in respect of this special function, sufficient to develop a firm basis for a contract between the executing agency and the client.

In such a case, the additional detail could be contained in an appendix to the POP – in fact, the proposed contract itself could be attached as an appendix if such a document had been prepared and used on previous projects. In any case, a contract will be required eventually, so why not produce it as early as possible? The outline may be established in the early versions of the POP and detail developed as the POP is expanded until a final contract is produced and is available when the plan of operation is completed and approved.

Even where a minimal POP is being employed or where the project is being run by the 'seat of the pants' method, some sort of order is required and certain factors have to be addressed, certain questions relative to the success of the project must be asked and answers produced.

Postulating that all POPs are dissimilar, nevertheless, they must all answer these certain basic questions. The most important questions are listed below; they should best be answered in the section of the POP indicated.

QUESTION	ANSWER – included in:
What will the project produce?	Goal; Purpose; Outputs; LFA; Description
Why is it required?	Background; LFA
Who will perform the work?	Strategy; Roles; Responsibilities; Organigram
How will the work be done?	Strategy; Organisation; Organigram; Activity Schedule; Responsibilities; LFA
When will it start and finish?	Schedule; Activity Matrix

How much will it cost?	Budget; Cash-flow; LFA
Where will it be done?	Location(s)
What can go wrong?	LFA; Strategy; Special Considerations

There are a certain few sections of the POP that answer **most** of these questions, at least in outline. The team should concentrate on them; the Logical Framework Analysis (LFA), Project Design Strategy, Organigram and Budget. The balance of the required information will follow easily when these sections have been developed.

PLAN OF OPERATION	Consultants
Contents	Associated Organisations
Table of Contents	Beneficiaries
Appendices	Reports
Abbreviations	Charts and Diagrams
	Activity/Responsibility Matrix
INTRODUCTION	Financial Procedures
Background	Approvals Procedure
Special Considerations	Payment Methodology
Logical Framework Analysis	Monitoring Schedule
Objectives	Implementation Schedule
	Reporting Schedule
DESCRIPTION OF THE PROJECT	Detailed Budget and Cash-flow
Location	Financial Approval Authorities
General Description	Approval Parameters
Project Design Strategy	Consultants
Financial	Contractors
Budget	Design
Source of funds	Evaluation
Cost control	
	APPENDICES
ORGANISATION AND CONTROL	Contracts
Organisation Chart	Consultant
Responsibilities and Roles	Contractor
Client	Financial Agreement
Staff	Mortgage Format

On the chart above are the 'contents' of a POP for an overseas low-cost housing project and give an idea of the essentials. Do not hesitate to expand or reduce the document according to your project or programme needs. An example of this sort cannot possibly cover all eventualities.

Of the previous 'contents', the most frequently omitted element is the 'Project Design Strategy'. It is important to the team to provide a strategy or planning rationale as an introduction to the thought that has generated the planning. Remember that the team membership may change, so strategy details are essential to the continuity of the project. In this strategy, describe why certain planning decisions have been made; indicate alternative sub-strategies and the circumstance that would initiate the alternatives. This is a narrative description and some non-technical phraseology may be introduced to make the rationalisation readily comprehensible to new team members and to upper management.

For very small or very fast projects, an organisation chart may serve as an abbreviated POP. Brief job descriptions may be written on the chart; alternatively, such a chart may comprise only a part of a POP and show a departmental organisation within a larger one. An example is given opposite for a Contracts Department within a larger project organisation. In this illustration there was also a full description of roles both within the POP and the procedures manual. The additional chart served as a quick guide for staff, other than Contracts Department staff, who found the procedures manual altogether too tedious. Try to avoid tedium; it disconcerts many an otherwise effective team member.

CONTRACTS DEPARTMENT

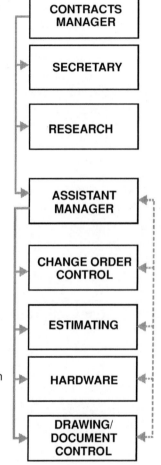

Supervision of contracts Department; advise other Departments as required. Reports to Project Manager — **CONTRACTS MANAGER**

Report to Contracts Manager — **SECRETARY**

Review contentious claims & make recommendations; assist in preparation of tender documents; resolve discrepancies in contract documents; provide technical support — **RESEARCH**

Define contract packages; prepare tender documents; answer tender queries; assist Contracts Manager; attend pre-tender & contract award meetings — **ASSISTANT MANAGER**

Initiate, receive, distribute change requests; liaise with estimators; maintain change records; advise on changes; assist Hardware section — **CHANGE ORDER CONTROL**

Estimate for changes; review change orders & contractor claims; other required estimating; material take-offs — **ESTIMATING**

Receive & distribute hardware; maintain quantity/cost records; liaise with suppliers & design group; recommend substitutions — **HARDWARE**

Control shop & record drawings; receive & issue contract documents; maintain contract document records — **DRAWING/ DOCUMENT CONTROL**

 'Planning, Logical Framework Analysis'

Planner

If providence smiles on you, if you are a lucky project manager, you will also be responsible for the planning; and therefore be your own 'Planner'. In the more often likely event that this is not so, the next best fall-back position is that the planner become and remain a member of the project team.

Given the improbability of either of these conditions, as soon as a project plan is received or, as soon as you are dropped into the middle of a planned project, your first step is to make a **thorough review of the plan of operation** or whatever other planning document or documents exist and which govern the implementation of the plan from that point forward – or the completion of the plan itself.

Expect expressions of outrage from everyone involved. But stick to your guns. Make it clear, preferably before but certainly immediately following acceptance of the project, that a review is essential and that a written report will be produced. If the team is already in place, it may be difficult to obtain unprejudiced views from all the members; they have probably been too close to the plan to view it critically and you may be asking them to change their minds – not an easy thing to do at the best of times.

So you may find yourself on your own – not unusual for an effective project manager. Review the supporting documentation (feasibility studies and the like), take the time you need for a proper appraisal, make such outside enquiries as might be required and such site visits as seem absolutely necessary. Do not be pressured into arriving at hasty conclusions. Call the report an 'accession report' or a similarly splendid title – that gives it more authority and credibility.

> ## Luck is not in the project manager's lexicon – 'Murphy's Law' is!

This is perhaps the ultimate example of how to avoid being made a scapegoat. However, when you decide that such a study and report are necessary and when you find little support, continue in the certainty that, should you fail to make an appraisal and recommend corrective actions, when things go wrong no-one will remember how bad the project probably was when you took over. Everyone may believe or pretend it is already the perfect project. But it is now **your** project and you are **fully responsible**. Blame for someone else's bad planning is one of the few certainties in the project management world.

The 'lucky' project manager, mentioned in the first paragraph, may be a small contractor or consultant who not only does his own planning and implementation but also cost control, monitoring, etc. For this one, there is no excuse if the project goes awry. It has always been your project and you are fully responsible from start to finish.

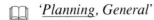 *'Planning, General'*

Procedures manual

For complex projects a procedures manual (giving all the details of interrelationships, activities, job descriptions, organigrams, procedure flow charts, financial procedures, etc.) will almost certainly be required. This **action** document is based on the plan of operation which is the **planning** document. Procedures manuals are often too complex for short-term projects but can be useful for a series of similar projects or a **programme** containing similar projects, especially if different personnel or outside consultants be employed. For programme/project-orientated organisations, a table of contents for a typical procedures manual is shown below. Many of the units will not be appropriate to your project but it gives an idea of the detail required and the types of activities and relationships to be included.

1.0 ORIGINS AND BACKGROUND

2.0 PROGRAM PHILOSOPHY
2.1 Introduction
2.2 Statement of Goals
2.3 Eligibility Criteria
2.4 Implementation Strategy
2.5 Contributions
2.6 Program Support
2.6.1   General
2.6.2   Needs Assessment
2.6.3   Training
2.6.4   Monitoring
2.6.5   Evaluation
2.6.6   Audit
2.6.7   Research

3.0 ORGANISATION
3.1 Organigram
3.2 The Program
3.3 Legal Status
3.4 Roles and Responsibilities
3.4.1   Task Force

3.4.2   Executing Agency
3.4.3   The Sponsor
3.4.4   Program Committee
3.4.5   Implementing Agency
3.4.6   Partner
3.4.7   Program Monitor

4.0 PROCEDURES
4.1 Application for Funds
4.2 Review and Approval
4.3 Agreement/Contract
4.4 Reporting
4.5 Monitoring
4.6 Project Completion
4.7 Project Evaluation by the
Executing Agency

5.0 FINANCE
5.1 Financial Context
5.2 Financial Accountability
5.3 Accounting Methods
5.4 Signing Authority
5.5 Program Income
5.6 Program Budget

It is important not to let the procedures manual become so complex that it be largely ignored, which, unfortunately may be the rule rather than the exception. In the case especially of a one-off/one project procedures manual, keep it short, keep it succinct. Use charts and diagrams to eliminate wordiness.

Experience will be the best guide in telling you how far to go in developing and formalising detailed procedures. Most project managers will err at least once in this respect, usually by producing too complex a document. However, do not neglect the statements of philosophy (2.1 to 2.4 in the example given) from which the actual procedures are derived. If a rational, intelligent group of officers know what their goal and purpose are supposed to be and how the requirements originated, common sense will dictate certain activities that will achieve the desired ends.

Procurement manual

Projects that involve mainly procurement and delivery of materials or equipment should have a manual in addition to and similar to the procedures manual – one that establishes without equivocation, who is responsible for which activity. Clear, graphically-legible flow charts of procurement procedures and approvals simplify the mechanisms. They should show, not only who is responsible for what activity but also monitoring intervention.

The procurement of materials is a very complex and specialised field. If the project has material procurement as a substantial element and there is no in-house expert, a consultant should be engaged. Let the consultant develop the procedures in the context of the team's requirements for planning scheduling and, especially, of **monitoring and reporting**. These last two procedures are as unlikely to be given their due importance by a procurement expert as by any other expert. Review the consultant's proposals and fit them into your own presentation plan. Remember the importance of charts and remember, too, that if it cannot be drawn logically on a flow chart then it cannot be done.

📖 *'Organisation, Procurement Manual'* and *'Communication, Charts and Diagrams'*

Project team

The project team may be large or small; it may – and often does – consist of the project manager alone. It may comprise delegated employees of departments in a larger organisation (the matrix) composed entirely of consultants or contract employees or be volunteer members of a professional organisation. There are so many possible permutations that only the concept can be properly addressed here; it is important above all that the project manger be more than just the 'nominal' leader of the team. Leadership implies authority; authority implies control.

Nevertheless, whatever its constituent parts, whatever its organisational philosophy, the attitude that is imparted (indoctrinated?) by the project manager is all important to its smooth operation. This is where the tact, patience and all those other essential qualities of the good project manager (PM) come into play and the PM learns the hardest lesson of all – managing people. She or he may also re-learn or become aware for the first time that the project manager usually has responsibility considerably greater than authority.

📖 *'Organisation, Project Team'* and *'Organisation, Aptitude'*

Project manager

Truly the key to the success of the project. There may be disagreement as to the qualities required to achieve that success and no more so than among project managers themselves. I have dared to suggest some of the qualities required, based mainly on personal experience but also some other writers' studies and observations. Whatever you may believe about these qualities and qualifications, a successful project manager has to be a notably different person than your functional manager.

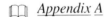 *'Organisation, Project Manager'*

Results

Project management by 'results' recognises a different **perspective** for the planning process and the interpretation of the benefits derived from the 'inputs'. 'Results' are those effects of the 'outputs' wherein behavioural changes induced by the outputs create different activities that generate the results desired, which in turn produce the purpose of the project (or goal at a higher level). 'Results' may also be seen as the productive operational activities that are made possible by the 'outputs' in combination or singly, plus their application.

For instance, a project of which three outputs are a clinic, pre-natal care equipment and a health-care-worker training course, may have as a 'result': local inhabitants have access to effective pre-natal health care services. 'Effective pre-natal health care services' are the result of the interaction of the physical outputs and the behavioural changes of the operators, effected by the training programme. The 'purpose' to which the 'outputs' and 'results' contribute could be to improve the infant survival rate in a certain location. 'Goal' would be more general, implying a general improvement in the health of the greater population of mothers and their children – in fact a synergistic result. If this seems a bit complex, that is because it is! But read it a couple of times and it makes sense. At least, it does to me. There is a revelatory chart and some more detail in Appendix A.

As a sweeping generalisation, most monitoring activities fail either because of their paucity or the frailties of the monitor. Monitoring and evaluating 'results' will test the skills of the planner and the monitor beyond the norm for customary evaluations. Those skills must be impeccable because the project will more readily founder due to personnel inadequacies.

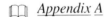 *Appendix A*

Schedule

Early group planning achieves cooperation that allows team members to establish their own schedule (within reasonable limits); as often as not, an optimistic one. This is much more effective than forcing associates into a pre-established scheduling strait-jacket – *and lays a guilt trip on them if they default.*

After proper discussion, encourage the team member or consultant to suggest his own time-frame. Usually, it will be optimistic; if it is not sufficiently so or is even pessimistic, be patient and discuss the timing reasonably until it approaches the requirements of the schedule. By this patient discussion and rationalisation, you are ensuring that the new time frame has been acknowledged as volunteered and not imposed; be certain it is perceived that way. This sort of discussion also serves genuinely as a review of the project and produces valid interpretations of both schedule and activities. It really is a useful exercise.

However, while 'optimistic' is acceptable in terms of the team member's own view of his contribution, note the warning; the time-frame must be realistic in terms of project development. It is not advocated that unrealistic projections be accepted, only that optimism be used to encourage maximum effort.

Never deliberately disguise or otherwise obscure your true schedule. Applying pressure to team members by setting unrealistic completion targets or by pretending to a progress different than the actual is always counterproductive. Eventually the scheduler loses the confidence of those being scheduled. What is more, should you be telling a different story to the client than to the team, there will eventually be a confusion as different information is exchanged at different levels between client and staff and your team. There is also the even greater danger that you, the project manager, will come to believe your own propaganda. If that happens then you are really in trouble! Do not forget that rational scheduling realistically takes into account all approval procedures (during implementation as well as during planning).

Do not provide others with opportunities or excuses for procrastination

---

There is a productivity curve for most projects, perhaps for all projects, which by the nature of management, people and circumstances rarely changes. The basic parameters of the curve are:

- 5% of production is achieved at 10% of project duration
- 95% of production is achieved at 80% of scheduled duration
- the last 5% of production takes 20% of the scheduled duration

The final two points are different ways of saying the same thing but the last axiom is the more explicit. During planning and implementation always keep in mind – the **last 5% of project production takes 20% of the time.**

Working to this criterion should enable the effective manager to close out with calm instead of panic. Considered in terms of cash-flow, the same principle applies. The last 5% of cash-flow (fees or contract price) generally comes due during, or at the end of, the last 20% of the project or contract schedule. If this aspect of cost control and scheduling has been properly considered and the project has been well managed there is no problem; but consider it during the **planning** phase or face the possibility of being cash-short during the last 20% of your schedule.

📖 *'Planning, Approvals'*

Strategic planning

Knowingly or unknowingly, project managers usually work within the context of a strategic plan. Of itself, this plan may not be of immediate and apparent importance to the practical execution of the project – but the project will certainly be important to the strategic plan. Project managers are so often up to their hips in alligators that the larger view loses immediate significance. For the operational manager, it is usually sufficient to know that the strategic plan exists and to be aware of its goals and how the project purpose may impact on the plan.

Should the project take a course that appears to contradict the goals of the strategic plan (SP), either during project planning or implementation, it should be brought to the attention of higher authority (the client). Perhaps the SP has changed and the information not been passed down the line. Or the plan of operation may have led in a direction other than that intended due to decisions made during implementation in order to respond to a crisis or to contend with new variables. The context of the SP should govern the project at all stages. Variations in the project should fit the SP or the SP should be modified if the client concludes that the changes in the project suggest an improved course for the governing programme.

Project evaluation is also an important factor in strategic planning. Ensure that the evaluation criteria and their method of presentation conform to the format and analytical framework already established in the strategic plan. If there is no such framework, the project manager has an obligation to recommend to the client that it be created.

📖 *'Monitoring, Monitoring & Strategic Planning'* and *'Communication, Feedback'*

Strategy (project design strategy)

In the plan of operation or work plan, it is important to include a project design strategy (PDS) or planning rationale as an introduction to the thought that has gone into the planning. In this strategy, describe why certain planning decisions have been made; indicate alternative sub-strategies and the circumstance that would initiate the alternatives. Others, reading the document at a later date, may not be immediately aware of your thought processes or all the factors that were considered. The PDS gives them an insight into the thoughts that produced the implementation scenario and makes it possible to anticipate what the original planner would have done under changed circumstances. Preferably this should be a narrative description. Specific, detailed data and undue precision is not expected. Make it informative, comprehensible and stimulating to read!

📖 *'Planning, Plan of Operation'*

Work breakdown structure

Apart from the obvious applications to scheduling, costing and contracting (see below), the work breakdown structure (WBS) serves as another guide to logical thought process. The term explains itself. Breaking the project down into rational components enables the planner to move them around, to classify them for assignment to team members in a responsibility/activity matrix, and to incorporate them into contracts for either implementation, supply or management objectives, depending on whether it is a thing or an activity, and to assign costs to the various parts or elements.

While, for example, it seems simple to analyse a vehicle as chassis, bodywork, engine, transmission, etc. and to develop sub-components of these, most **projects** do not fit this simplistic scheme. However, it is worth the trouble of creating a WBS for most projects and the more obscure classifications may be simplified by using the Logical Framework Analysis chart as a base from which to develop the analysis. Some certainty can be derived at least from the levels of input and output, with the principal problem occurring at purpose level; in one analogy, 'purpose' might correspond to vehicle and 'goal' the use to which one would put a fleet of vehicles. A series of 'purposes' (vehicles) lead to the 'goal' (fleet).

Alternatively, one could consider a 'programme' as being the top line (a single element) of the WBS, followed by the 'projects' that comprise the programme at the second level. Below that (third level) are outputs and at the lower of four levels are the inputs. These inputs could be broken down even further into 'tasks' or 'activities' or smaller units of the inputs, giving a fifth level. If, for instance, funding is to be provided as an input by a Non-Governmental Organisation (NGO) then the amount required would be shown at Level 4. Below that (level five), the funding could be broken down into the activities that will generate the funding such as:

- fund-raising plan
- seeking volunteers
- printing circulars
- television advertising
- *and many other activities.*

All these activities can be costed either as a composite of NGO staff time plus overheads or as actual disbursements from NGO funds. At the same time, responsibility can be assigned for the different activities. The levels would appear as follows:

Level 1	Program	Level 4	Inputs
Level 2	Projects	Level 5	Activities
Level 3	Outputs		

This latter is probably the more practical application of the WBS both for planning and implementation; it also lends itself readily for inputting into most project management computer programs. A diagram is given as an example for a small house construction in Appendix E. Remember that the principle is applicable to any sort of project.

📖 *Appendix E, 'Work Breakdown Structure'*; *'Organisation, Responsibility, Responsibility/activity Matrix'*

PROJECT MANAGEMENT FAILURE CRITERIA

The unrecognised and usually unacknowledged factors that often explain why the project does not proceed as the client thinks it should.

- My convenience is more important than that of the client.

- We have that contract; now we have lots of time and money to get another.

- Postpone the crisis; tell the client anything that will shut him up.

- Scheduled completion? Tell him ..... finished next week.

- I've been doing this for twenty years; what does the he think he knows about it?

- Don't answer the phone; it may be someone I don't want to talk to.

- I'm busy with the project; I don't have time to sit and compose letters.

- I thought Fred had taken care of that already.

TAKE A BREAK

2

Organisation

The project manager, aptitude and the matrix

Aptitude

It goes without saying that you need the right person for the right job, that you don't want a square peg in a round hole and all the other bromides but it isn't always achievable ... and in any case, when project management is proposed or adopted within a large organisation, some functional managers have other priorities that impede logical selection for a matrix team.

Of course, the happy project manager is the one that is allowed to select his team members. **But, there are not many happy project managers.**

Ideally as well as common-sensically, in establishing a team roster, it is at least important, and I say essential, to write the job description and fit the person to it rather than the reverse.

> *A construction/project manager on a multi-million dollar project, spent two and a half years trying to develop an organisation chart and job descriptions that would suit the staff he selected. Unfortunately, what with people quitting and new ones being hired, he was never able to complete either – the job was finished without a chart. This really happened – which, you may believe, proves that organigrams are unnecessary. Not, however, if you had worked there!*

This may not be the only example you will find in this book of things you don't need to be told, that are so obvious that everyone must do it. But it happens all too often that available personnel are either bullied and shaped into a position or, even worse, the job description is modified to suit the available staff. This a sure way to mutilate the project. Avoid it to the best of your ability. Ignore pressure within the organisation to adapt to what you will be told are the 'practicalities'. Write the job descriptions with an eye, solely, to the needs of the project; otherwise the project will suffer. At least start with the proper criteria; give yourself a sound base from which to depart if the pressures become irresistible. And, a warning that you will find frequently in these pages, make sure your proposed job descriptions are well and truly recorded and instructions to 'adapt' to other requirements are equally registered.

In selecting team personnel, when you find yourself between the proverbial rock and the hard place, if you do not have control of the selection procedure, if all technical and professional requirements cannot be met in staffing, if you are limited to available personnel, unable to contract outside personnel, it is essential that, as a minimum, the **philosophical and personality qualities** of the candidate suit the position.

This means, desirably, the proposed team member have an enthusiasm for, or at least a ready acceptance of, the principles of project management, of the matrix and of the spirit of cooperation essential to the well-functioning team. It also means that such a candidate should be prepared to admit to a degree of inadequacy **in this particular matrix position** and be more than usually willing to accept constructive questioning and helpful suggestions from team members.

On that last-mentioned design/build project with twenty or more interrelated contracts extant at any one time, a major requirement that I constantly emphasised was the need for capable inspectors of trades. The skills required by this once-omnipresent 'clerk of the works' are specialised technical knowledge in one or more building trades and, even more important, the ability to interpret contracts and specifications.

Jim, was a veritable genius in the field. He knew every detail of every trade. I had worked with him and learned a great deal from him. For which reason, I enthusiastically recommended him for a senior inspection position. The Construction/project Manager was so overwhelmed by Jim's expertise that he appointed him as his Assistant with responsibility for coordinating and scheduling all the work.

> *Jim, accustomed to working for architects and engineers; accustomed to saying 'stop the work!' if he found an error; accustomed, too, to dismissing a man from the site if he arrived without a safety helmet, could not readily change his spots.*
>
> *Over the next few months he set scheduling deadlines that could not be and were not met. Being on the inside was a lot different from being on the outside with the power and authority of the client. The result was a degree of chaos until Jim quit in frustration. Square pegs in round holes don't work.*

In the case of the project manager particularly, because the required skills depend so much on these parameters (philosophy and personality), a good, well-chosen **project manager** may more readily switch talents between sectors and function effectively, on condition there be available to him or her team members with the required technical and/or professional expertise. To a lesser extent, this has to apply to all members of the team when chosen from within an existing organisation, with the degree of variance in requirement depending on the importance of the technical and/or professional attributes that the team member brings to the project.

📖 *'Monitoring, Inspection (Construction)'* and *'Organisation, Project Manager'*

Authority

Authority, to be effective, must be in the proper hands. It is no use being a project manager if you are not allowed to manage. This will be one of the principal difficulties that you will face in all your work. There is always someone who knows better how the job should be done *(and, worse, sometimes is right!)*. All too often it is your superior – which makes things more than modestly difficult, even challenging.

The problem is to maintain good relations with the boss (the client) without being sycophantic, keep the project functioning properly, and get it completed according to its planned terms and schedule. This is no easy task. If you **know** your method is the right one, go ahead and do it but in the full knowledge of the potential for discord if you are overruled. The proof is found in the results. At the same time extend yourself to the maximum to create a fall-back position in case you receive a specific instruction to do it some other way. If that does happen (an instruction contrary to your best advice), make sure the instruction is **recorded**, either in a memo or minutes. Of course, no matter what the circumstances, you must accept full responsibility for your actions. You may do something unwelcome because you feel you have to. In fact you do have a choice; a difficult one. You can always refuse and accept the consequences.

Don't worry about losing the occasional test of convictions. It is the project manager's lot to be opposed and you can't win all the time. There is also the justifiable situation, from management's or the clients point of view, where other imperatives of 'goal' override those of 'purpose'. In a large organisation such as a government department, 'goal' may change dramatically overnight to fulfil a higher policy initiative. In such a case, you are wrong, period – so accept with good grace.

📖 *'Responsibility, Authority'*

Charts and diagrams

Most aspects of organisation are more readily illustrated by charts and diagrams than by verbal description. The basic organigram (organisation chart), with some added notes, may be all that is required for the simplest project organisation; more complex projects will have organigrams within organigrams. For example, a large and complex departmental organigram that is represented by only one box on the basic organigram may have as much detail within itself as the overall diagram. There are also implementation schedules, monitoring schedules and so on. There is more information in other sections, especially 'Communication' wherein charts and diagrams are considered as effective communication tools – with some examples.

📖 *'Communication, Charts & Diagrams'* and *'Planning, Charts & Diagrams'*

Committee

Committees seem to be an inevitable concomitant of management and organisation within a bureaucracy. They *can* be a mechanism, albeit a cumbersome one, for solving a problem but much more often are used to postpone or avoid a decision. **Teams**, on the other hand, are created to get things done. The virtue of the team is that it has a leader with authority *(well, some authority ... well, some of the time!)*.

While the well-chosen, well-run team theoretically will (in a perfect world) arrive at conclusions by consensus, in case of disagreement, there is always a fall-back position. **The project manager makes the decision** and gets action. It is essential that this be the case, otherwise the team, which is there to expedite and complete the project, will simply become another headless committee devoting itself to profound discussion, postponement of action and perpetuation of itself. Risky stuff, perhaps, but how else will you complete the project?

Do not let the *team* become a *committee*

Because the committee is usually the offspring of the large bureaucratic organisation (government, multi-national, etc.), small organisations need not concern themselves with it unduly. The independent consultant project manager, should use her/his wiles to forestall their creation in any organisation for which s/he is working. If they are an unavoidable part of the work environment, consider how the delays they cause may affect your fee structure and your time schedule and adjust them accordingly.

A one-person 'team' is usually more effective than a committee

---

In planning and implementation, the project manager should avoid the committee procedure wherever possible. If it cannot be avoided, follow (or at least recommend) these guidelines in the creation of the body:

- as few members as possible – three is enough
- if more expertise is required, employ consultant or departmental experts advising the committee rather than expand the committee
- terms of reference must be entirely clear – no roaming into other jurisdictions
- define clear reporting procedures
- appoint a strong chairman
- require detailed minutes of proceedings
- establish schedules for production of recommendations on a phased basis
- nominate an overriding authority should the committee fail to comply with any of its terms of reference, meet the schedule or fail to produce firm recommendations
- in the case of an independent, paid committee, impose an **inviolable** budget limitation on its activities.

As an alternative to establishing a committee or sub-committee, try appointing one person (a committee of one or an Assistant Project Manager) to perform the task, with clearly defined access, embodied in the terms of reference, to other team members or to outside assistance. Make that person fully responsible for the particular task, investigation, proposal, or whatever, reporting back to the project team in a specific time-frame. Monitor the process to make sure that cooperation is fully extended to the responsible person by all others involved in the operation.

Such a situation may be suitable for the employment of a consultant, provided always that there be proper terms of reference, a strict contract with a time-frame and, for preference, a fixed, lump-sum contract price. (With a lump-sum contract, you as the client must be careful to be specific as to requirements [terms of reference] and absolutely fair in managing the contract. Otherwise you may never get the consultant again and the word will get around that the client is too demanding. There may also be justifiable claims for extra payment which are difficult to refute and more than a little embarrassing.)

> *There was (and probably still is) an important government department that wrote critical letters by committee. The draft was presented at a meeting of some twenty people; they discussed it, took it away and commented in writing. Then they met again to review the document and another draft was made ... and so on. This is possibly the worst-case example of the futility of the committee and of its potential for procrastination – but, sadly, common practice.*

In most cases, the use of an individual (staff member or consultant) is much more effective than going the committee route; it puts the person on his/her mettle by assigning unequivocal responsibility.

Should the results of the task, perhaps a report or its conclusions, be unacceptable to the team, at least there should now be enough information for the team to reach a conclusion of its own, assuming that the person was well-chosen and the task properly described. In the event of employment of a consultant, an indisputably inadequate report may be rejected and additional work called for at no increase in cost. In such a case the committee and the project manager must be very certain of their reasons for rejection.

> *I was elected Chairman of a four-person entertainment committee, at the first meeting. We were supposed to choose movies for the month (12 in all). After 3 hours, we hadn't selected one or even decided on the parameters for choice. I prorogued the meeting and never called another. I was Chairman for a year, selected all the movies (over 140), arranged bingo, dances, imported orchestras and organised all the other entertainment. I didn't please everyone but at least the 2,500 members knew who was responsible. Never heard from the other committee members again! 'Arrogant' do you think? Maybe, but sometimes desperate situations call for desperate measures.*

A possible exception to these strictures against committees is the 'Executive Committee' (ExecCom). Usually this comprises nominated members of a larger committee which acts within a broad policy framework, originated by the committee as a whole, to interpret their policy recommendations or decisions (depending on the committee's level of authority) into action.

If the ExecCom consists of no more than three members and if they meet frequently, there is a fair chance of getting something done. A single manager is preferred but, if not permitted for whatever political reason, an executive group within a committee is a rational and acceptable alternative.

A brief advisory for small organisations. Although I say above that they need not worry about committees, their problems are often an **absence** of committees or, at least, of the discipline that a small committee must follow. Partners often get together to kick around ideas. In effect they are functioning as a committee and should establish some norms for discussion. One person should be appointed to take notes and ensure that everyone has agreed to the decisions taken and that they are formally stated – this avoids later accusations of 'I'm sure you said …' or 'That's not how I remember it'. Needless (or perhaps needful) to say, the notes should be entered somewhere into the record system. A lot of friendships have been shattered because of different interpretations of agreements casually made.

📖 *'Planning, Approvals'* and *'Communication, Meetings'*

Computer

Computer technology has been a boon to project management but, while it may enhance the art or science of project management, it cannot replace it. Do not allow the technology to become more important than the exercise.

There will be no shortage of experts to tell you that you need more sophisticated programs or any shortage of staff looking for the latest toys. Project management is still a matter of logic and common-sense; we have not yet reached the stage when this will be replaced by a machine *(not quite yet)*. Use only the mechanical, electronic and technological aids that you **need**; do not be overawed by the patina of sophistication that computers seem to lend to management.

When developing a special computer program to meet certain needs, it is proper that the programmers consult all potential beneficiaries to determine inputs and outputs. But care is required by management in the decision as to how many interests the program shall serve.

No computer program can be all things to all people. The attempt to satisfy everybody will usually lead to a plethora of useless information. This has happened more than once, ending with reports that are too complex to be read, useful information buried under mountains of paper. We all know of computer systems that were established at enormous cost only to be abandoned in a very short time when found to either produce too much, too little or too costly data. This can apply equally to systems of enormous scope or to small office systems.

When contemplating the use of either a total system or a new program, first determine what information is required, what purpose it will serve and how much may be spent on it. Try to rein in the enthusiasm of the computer whiz. Decide how much a computer program can save, how much it may generate in additional income and, consequently, how much you may spend. A proper budget will usually produce a suitable program or a suitable system. (A 'proper' budget would be a phased budget with certain capability criteria to be met at each stage of program development before stage approval and the release of a further disbursement – and, of course, disbursements that fit into the company's strategic budget plan.)

This caution applies equally to off-the-shelf programs. They are being constantly 'improved' to serve a wider user clientele until they become unwieldy, require more sophisticated and expensive hardware and are often, indeed usually, employed to the extent of only a small percentage of their capacity. It too often happens that one gradually and unconsciously acquires a system that could be of enormous benefit if only you had the time to study it but which takes so long to save your work or produce an answer that it is a constant irritant. This warning applies mostly to the small two or three-person business operation that cannot ignore the snapping alligators long enough to take a course in the use of the software. It becomes more critical as the business grows and takes on more staff and more technology, beyond the capacity of the personnel's learning curve.

But neither do I, nor should you, deprecate the computer. It would be difficult today to contemplate running a complex project without the assistance of this sophisticated tool. Just keep the beast under control. And take the time, at least, to learn to manage thoroughly that part of the technology that you may usefully employ. Learning obscure and rarely-used functions is a waste of time and they soon fade from one's memory.

Of course, this is pretty basic stuff. We hope that any management innovation is considered in terms of its objective, its costs and its likelihood of improving the project, the system, the bottom line, etc.

📖 *'Communication, Computer'*; and anecdote under *'Contracts, Specifications'*

Control

Remember always that **whoever controls the money, controls the project**. This concept is an essential criterion of your organisational philosophy if you wish to generate a proper planning psychology for effective control of the project. Your organisational structure must clearly establish who has authority in financial matters and the scope accorded to each element of that financial control. Ultimately it must all lead to final control being in the hands of the project manager who reports to a 'client'. The 'client' (whether inside or outside your organisation) is, of course, the supreme boss from the project manager's point of view and has the ultimate 'control' in being able to stop the project by stopping the money.

Do not take this matter of control lightly. 'Control' is not a dirty word. Do not allow yourself to be persuaded that it is either an 'undemocratic' or 'belligerent' concept. To make a project run as it should, some element of pressure on all the parties concerned is required. The only effective one is money *(although when the going gets really rough, you may sometimes think that a club would be more effective)*.

The project manager may not be always in the ideal position of having full control of this essential element (in fact, that is the exception rather than the rule) but, whatever your situation, take this very important reality into account in your planning. Inevitably, someone else's hands on the purse strings will impact detrimentally on your effectiveness.

📖 *'Communication, Charts & Diagrams – Organigram'*; *'Responsibility, Control'*; *'Responsibility, Ethics, Client'* and *'Planning, Control'*

DoList

Despite the ubiquity of electronic recording, there is nothing that quite replaces an old-fashioned piece of squared or lined paper. You don't have to boot up a computer or scroll or whatever. There it is in neat or untidy columns, all visible at one glance, marked with your own special hieroglyphics but immediately understood.

Always have a DoList (your own action sheet) on your desk with a list of things to be done in the next few days. This should remain on your desk at all times. Cross off each item as it is completed (do not obliterate it completely – you may have to refer to it again); if the completed action generates a new action, write that on the list and if it is farther in the future, note it in the diary at an appropriate future date.

As the DoList is completed, copy the remaining items onto a new sheet and start again; **file** the discarded DoLists – do not throw them away. Some current diaries have special sheets for this system. **No essential action should be omitted from the DoList.** But, at the same time, try to keep it to one sheet of paper (better make it A4 size).

This may be another occasion when you ask 'how many project managers (or other managers, for that matter) are there that don't already do this'? The answer is that most do not. It is an absurdly simple procedure (some may think simple-minded) and perhaps may be too suggestive of personal inadequacy for the unjustifiably self-confident manager. Risk any derision this DoList might occasion; it is an old-fashioned but effective technique. The size of the organisation within which you operate has nothing to do with the effectiveness of the DoList; the DoList is for yourself alone. But a one-woman or one-man organisation may find it more useful than most – there is no-one else to tell you that you have missed something.

📖 *'Communication, Diary'*

Management

One dictionary definition of management is 'the judicious use of means to achieve an end'. This is exactly what **project management** is all about. Although, in containing a modifier (project), the term may suggest something less than 'management' in the complete sense, all the **techniques** that apply to project management apply equally to generic or functional management.

The changeling from project management to functional management may find that targets tend to move around more – generally, of course, the transition is the other way. 'Goals' or 'objectives' in functional management are seen as more flexible than 'purposes' in project management. The imperatives of working in direct contact with outside influences rather than those contained **within** the goal orientation, require flexibility of response at the level of 'goal'. But, if you have mastered project management, functional management should not be unnerving. An adjustment has to be made in terms of flexibility just as a transfer from functional management to project management compels an adjustment in terms of doggedness, single-mindedness, and **commitment to the project.**

It is often the case, and especially for non-governmental organisations, independent consultants and small construction contractors, that a project is the first step in the creation of a new functional organisation. In providing assistance to establish a new organisation or a new element of an existing organisation, a project is the obvious means. When designing the project, take into account the need for that organisation or element to continue its operations; consider the transition from project to function. Do the same staff that develop the project continue in the functional establishment? If not, have the handover procedures been properly considered? Does the project plan have job descriptions for the new staff and an employment procedure? .... and so on.

> **A project manager need not be technically competent in the subject of the project**

Matrix management

The adoption and advocacy of matrix management by large organisations and government departments has established it as the norm for project management. However, most of the precepts and techniques recommended in this book apply equally to projects under most other forms of control. The matrix, in other words, is not a *sine qua non* of successful project management.

As an example, the independent consultant project manager (consultant) who provides a total team to a client may be assured of an even greater possibility of project success in not being required to give consideration to the requirements of functional management in a rigid organisation; this dichotomy of priorities (between 'functional' and 'project' management) is often the most difficult problem that the in-house project manager has to cope with. For which reason, those requirements of diplomacy in the character of the project manager will probably be most exercised when interacting with a functional manager who considers that he or she has 'lost' a good employee to assignment within a matrix. Even worse, the employee might feel the same way and may require a little stroking before accepting the new status.

📖 '*Organisation, Project Team*' and '*Responsibility, Authority*'

Organigram

There is no doubt in my mind (and I hope you will come to agree) that the organigram (organisation chart) is the project manager's most useful tool. The organigram, although usually acknowledged as a 'requirement', is not often accorded the respect it deserves. **Properly considered and completed**, it forms the basis for a multitude of logical conclusions that assist in developing and implementing the project.

The organigram can, should – indeed must (or fail in its purpose):

- delineate authority
- indicate true control
- define relationships
- assist in developing role definitions
- demonstrate requirements for contracts
- clarify reporting requirements
- show money flow – by showing 'control'.

It may do all these things and more but only if it is considered, and considered seriously, as a useful tool to be developed **at the earliest possible moment** and not as something that is drawn, in a hurry, as a bothersome adjunct of the project plan. There is more information in the section 'Communication, Charts and Diagrams'.

📖 '*Communication, Charts & Diagrams*'

Organigram as a POP

For simple and short-term projects, the organigram alone may be annotated and expanded to supply most of the essential information that is usually contained in a plan of operation (POP). This is covered in more detail in the 'Planning' section and an example is given.

📖 *'Planning, Plan of Operation'*

Procedures manual

This is the 'gospel' according to the project manager. Make sure that everyone knows exactly what they are doing and how it should be done. Unfortunately, procedures manuals often become so complex as to be ignored and only referred to when something has obviously gone wrong – usually too late. Remember in this context that the value of a chart or organigram is that it can simplify the understanding of a procedure; so make sure that, wherever possible in the procedures manual, a diagram replaces or usefully complements the text. Such a manual is equally important to the functional manager of either small or large enterprises. It is surprising how many managers feel it is not necessary to explain why and how things should be done.

📖 *'Planning, Procedures Manual'* and *'Procurement Manual'*

Procurement manual

For a project that is concerned exclusively with procurement, the procedures manual may be replaced or complemented by a procurement manual. Inevitably, the procurement manual, if attached to the procedures manual, may become the primary document that determines the effectiveness of the project. There is also a massive inescapability about procedures set in motion for large procurement projects that limits alternatives and remedial action in a most alarming way. The procedures manual cannot afford to be wrong. Different people are using it in different environments and often widely-distanced places; if the elements do not come together as they should, chaos results.

The procurement manual, in that it may replace the procedures manual as the daily reference manual, should contain all the pertinent documents that govern the procurement procedures, such as purchasing contracts, the terms of reference of consultant contracts, the key elements of any intergovernmental or intra-company agreements, the roles and responsibilities of the chief participants, spending authorities, etc.

Again, charts and diagrams are still the best way to illustrate the procedures required for complex procurement but they tend to become complicated if too many procedures are combined in one chart. It may be necessary to separate ordering and delivery from approvals and payments in related, similar charts with references in each one to the other or any other arrangement that simplifies understanding of operations.

📖 '*Planning, Procurement Manual*'

Project manager

Study of the management recommendations throughout this manual should give a clear indication of the qualifications required of the accomplished project manager. If the project manager (PM) could do all the things required of him or her, that would presuppose perfection.

Though conceding the expectation of falling a little short of perfection, at least strive for it in your work and expect the same degree of effort of the team. But do not expect more of the team than you are prepared to offer in all the required characteristics of dedication, integrity, punctuality, respect, tact, and all those praiseworthy qualities outlined below. A good PM is the key to a successful project, large or small. There are probably as many opinions of the essential qualifications for a first-rate PM as there are definitions of the term itself. As different special interest groups redefine the English language, so now anyone, at any level of expertise, can be a 'project manager'. (The Project Management Institute [USA] is the only body I know of that solely represents project managers in the way that architectural institutes represent architects).

However, if we consider that a project manager is one who needs to understand the procedures and methods that define a project and must carry the project from mental sketch to drawing board to concrete existence, generally, but not always, within a matrix environment, then the qualities and experience listed below must be required.

Attitude

The proper **attitude** is a composite of many of the qualifications summarised below. It is essential to approach the requirements of project management and those of each project with the certain conviction that the project is yours to succeed or to fail and to accept full responsibility for its success or failure; the **success of the project being paramount**. *This is an easy enough concept for the individual promoting, planning and executing a project for him or herself or as a sole project manager to a client but requires a special determination when operating inside a larger organisation.*

A common impediment to developing this 'proper' attitude is the personal and human need one feels to be oneself, to express one's personality, to demand the privileges of position, often to the detriment of project effectiveness. But, if established plans and methods are flouted by the PM in order to satisfy a whim, an emotional fulfilment or to resolve the immediate crisis in which one finds oneself or if the 'I have always done it this way' syndrome is allowed, even momentarily, to rule over reason and logic, then the project is at risk.

There is a real danger in what I call 'management by charisma'. People with charm and of forceful personality can often be found in project management (or other management) positions, doing things 'their' way and succeeding to the extent that the charm prevails over logic, dragging the team along by sheer force of personality.

But eventually there will be an accounting. Either the pressure will be too much for the team and the individuals will suffer burn-out or the jumping from crisis to crisis will jeopardise this or an associated project by the postponing of deadlines. A certain amount of justifiable animosity towards the PM will also be an inevitable result.

It is essential to subjugate your idiosyncrasies to the needs of the project; never your dedication. Always maintain your dedication but try to control your whims.

Communication

Just as communication is the essence of good project management, so is the ability to communicate fundamental to the project manager. This means that the PM must be:

- a good listener – communication is a two-way street
- articulate without being garrulous
- literate – people really do need to know what you are talking about
- straightforward, forthright
- precise
- prompt – delayed communication equals no communication.

Analytical ability

The essence of project management is to take a plethora of information and turn it into a plan and a project. This requires the ability to convert concepts and circumstances into practical components by a logical thought process. The project manager must be able to remove him/herself from the pressures of the moment, sit back and follow a process or procedure, rationally, from beginning to end, considering also all those outside influences that impact on that process.

Very few people have the ability to return to first principles. This is a great asset for a project manager – to be able to cut away extraneous accumulations of data and misconceptions and return to the essence of what

> *An oft-cited example of returning to first principles is the case of a manufacturer that planned to build a new warehouse to store its products. The consultant project manager, instead of immediately calling in architects and engineers, reviewed the client's operations. The result was a change in shipping and scheduling methods that obviated the need for a new warehouse. Every project cannot be resolved this way but the antecedents and the context of the project should be thoroughly analysed before charging ahead.*

Toughness

The generous and honest use of authority for the benefit of the client and the project is essential. Although I have repeatedly stated that the project manager usually does not have authority to match responsibility, he or she still exercises substantial influence over people and events. This influence should be applied with:

- decisiveness
- consideration for others
- exclusively to the benefit of the project and, thus, the client.

Organisation

The project manager must be inherently well organised as a fact of his or her normal everyday existence. One cannot put on a cloak of organisation if it is not part of one's personal reality. So the project manager must be:

- punctual
- punctilious
- diligent
- expeditious
- a good manager of time
- able to delegate effectively
- prepared for tedium.

Personality

Personality traits are a large part of the natural equipment of a good project manager. Some of these traits may be irritating to others in the normal exercise of social intercourse (may drive you crazy!) but they most effectively serve a purpose when applied to project management. Some major ones are:

- common-sense(ical)
- intuitive – understands people and their motivations
- calm – controls his or her emotions
- decisive – without being aggressive
- inherently orderly
- considerate
- patient
- tenacious, resolute, determined
- tactful
- prefers persuasion and negotiation
- fastidious
- naturally frugal without being miserly
- content with the inner satisfaction of a job well done.

Although project managers may not be born, as are artists, the nuances of their personality and their educational background and experience have a pronounced effect on their capability.

> **Ask yourself ... is it more important to indulge your personal idiosyncrasies than to complete a successful project?**

Before the popularisation of specialisation in architectural studies, the key element of training that made a successful architect was a combination of analytical thinking and the requirement for coordination between design and construction specialists, leading to a logical project implementation. Given all the other personality qualifications, an architect so trained and **with his feet on the ground** potentially made one of the best project managers. On the other hand, the architect with charismatic design capability but a paucity of common-sense may well be the worst.

📖 *'Organisation, Aptitude'*

Project team

General

Although most of the guidelines in this manual apply broadly and equally to any management methodology, generally they are founded on the premise that project teams are composed of members selected to form a matrix within a functional management environment.

There are professionals who believe this is not the best method, that the matrix team interferes with normal functional management to a degree that jeopardises working relationships. This may be true for some organisations and for some individuals but the matrix has proven itself for many others.

Assuming that there is a specific need for a team, in establishing the team roster, it is important to write the job description first and fit the person to it. As mentioned under 'Aptitude', it often happens that available personnel are either dragooned into unsuitable positions or the job description is modified to fit the qualifications and experience of personnel chosen by default. I reiterate that the job description must be developed **solely to serve the needs of the project**. In the matrix environment, it is usually possible to employ team members from within the functional organisation on a project duration basis or suitable consultants may be employed as required.

In any event, the job descriptions **must** be applicable to a variety of employment possibilities such as the contracting of outside consultants, secondment of personnel from another department or hiring of new staff on a short-term basis.

In selecting team personnel, when circumstances place you between the proverbial rock and the hard place in the selection of staff from within an existing organisation, if all technical and professional requirements cannot be met in staffing, it is essential, at least, that the **philosophical and personality** qualities of the candidate suit the position.

This means that the person have a ready acceptance of the principles of project management, of the matrix and of the spirit of cooperation essential to the well-functioning team. The matrix candidate who does not completely fill the position requirements may expect to find the initiation to **this particular matrix position** to be difficult and should anticipate and accept constructive advice from other team members and, especially, from the project manager. The project manager must take special care in this situation to ensure that the maximum contribution is extracted from the team member without diminishing his or her effectiveness because of reservations of other team members.

📖 *'Organisation, Project Team, Personnel Selection'*

Consultants

There may be some bias detectable in my strong recommendation of the employment of consultant or contract workers in preference to full-time staff as project team members. There are advantages and disadvantages. I believe the former outweigh the latter; in fact, there are very few disadvantages if it is done properly. The following factors should be considered.

- It is more probable that a consultant can be selected who has all the required qualifications rather than requiring that a staff member adapt to certain special conditions.

- The project manager has greater control in that there is no functional (line) management reporting requirement to conflict with the consultant's project duties and the project objectives.

- The amount of time required to be devoted to the project can be established and **demanded** of the consultant as a term of the employment contract.

- A tightly written contract, in conjunction with the job description, can establish clear, enforceable performance criteria.

- Initial cost of a consultant may **appear** higher; it usually isn't if all considerations of overhead (office space, vacation, sickness, workers compensation, pension, etc.) are taken into account.

- Should the consultant, at some time, prove unacceptable, it is much easier (with a proper contract) to remove him or her and get a replacement.

The reason this method is used less than it should be lies perhaps in the second consideration listed above. A great deal more authority is conferred on the project manger than in the traditional matrix arrangement. Simultaneously, the power of functional management is reduced in proportion to the number of consultants that are employed and the number of permanent staff not, thereby, required. In a bureaucratic environment, employment of consultants may be reluctantly conceded but is not likely to gain acceptance as a matter of general policy. *Despite functional management's habitual dislike of matrix management, it is, in fact, usually found more acceptable than any alarming alternative that could permanently diminish functional management's scope and authority.*

The ideal management system for the new millennium is probably that of a skeleton organisation with a minimum of experienced officers controlling a work-force comprised largely of contracted consultant personnel. One would need to employ a higher level of expert, full-time staff specifically qualified to negotiate contracts and review, comprehend and measure the value of the work produced. Maybe I make that last qualification sound easy; it is not.

In this scenario, officers would be responsible for establishing terms of reference and for monitoring performance and budget. The need for a vast middle-level management would be diminished; full-time support staff would be mostly engaged on contract preparation and administration.

The flexibility inherent in such a system would enable the organisation to respond quickly to outside influence and would generate substantial cost savings. This is not a new idea; some government departments have already begun the process but governments and business generally are probably not prepared to see it as a major policy shift in running most of their project operations.

What may also happen and what may at first seem cumbersome is that the permanent staff, employing a consultant to perform a specific task, may not have the technical expertise to judge performance and may not have this capacity available in another full-time employee. The solution is to employ a second consultant to monitor the first consultant. Somewhere along the line a certain amount of trust is involved. The second consultant has to be reputable to a degree that invites that trust. I have been contracted in this 'monitoring consultant' position both short-term and long and I assure you that it works. Note my stress on monitoring; it recurs throughout this manual. It is difficult to exaggerate its importance.

Personnel selection

In a matrix format, the project manager will find him/herself with little choice in selecting members for the project team. This problem, already alluded to above, may be compounded in the bureaucratic environment by the inherent unsuitability of the person as a member of the team or even as an employee of the department involved. If the functional manager of the department has been landed, by whatever, process with a square peg, he or she is liable to see the project team as the round hole into which to plug the unfortunate employee. In fact the team could, and often does, become the burial ground of a host of unlucky, unwanted people.

As background to this dilemma it is worth considering how bureaucrats (in the widest use of the term) get to be where they are. First let me say that both the public service as I knew it and private industry, too, were filled with more than a few clever, keen, hard-working people. The major problem facing bureaucracy was, and probably still is the rules and regulations governing advancement. The 'Peter Principle' stipulates that people rise in a bureaucracy to their level of incompetence. This level is, of course different for each individual. But a competent worker, doing excellent work at a certain level of expertise, can be rewarded financially only within a limited range. Having reached that salary maximum, it is essential to move up a classification in order to increase earnings. Cramming for a test for the next level is not that difficult and a good many useful people thus rise out of their area of expertise and comfort – finding themselves then in a work environment that they cannot manage. At this stage they become a burden and candidates for a sideways transfer or secondment to the matrix team – sad but often true. There is an answer to this problem but it involves a major shift in industry and workplace philosophy. It is reward for performance rather than longevity – unlikely in this or the next century.

If, within your company or other bureaucratic environment you are allowed to conduct a genuine search for team members, take note that recommendations from a person's superior are not always well motivated nor are they based on the same perceptions as those of the person's inferiors. An employee may reveal one facade to a superior and another to those he or she directs. Discreet enquiries of those underlings often reveal a totally different person to the one who has received glowing performance reports for any number of years.

Confrontation

Confrontation is contrary to the spirit of project management. If you think this is insufficient reason for avoiding it, consider also that it **usually** fails to give beneficial results.

However, the cool, calm, collected project manager (PM) who is noted for his or her rational and considerate approach may, on rare occasions, use aggressive confrontation as a considered tool to obtain compliance. There are some specific prerequisites for this technique. The PM must be absolutely sure of being absolutely correct. The recalcitrance (or whatever) that is to be overcome must have been sufficiently persistent and overt to have been observed by the rest of the team or other players in the situation, sufficient to give validity to the PM's contemplated action, indeed, even to make it welcome to the other team members.

On the assumption that the confrontation is a corrective measure, then it is best 'performed' in the presence of one but preferably only one observer (this reduces the potential resentment by limiting positive knowledge of the subject's reprimand – the victim will not talk and the witness will not be believed). If an absolutely crushing confrontation is required with no hope of redemption for the crushed, then a wide audience is preferable. The consequence is the preclusion of any future cooperation from the miscreant and will likely be followed by either his/her resignation or, of necessity, removal from the project. A meeting is a useful place for this latter exercise. However, should you be wrong, should the supposed sinner have a ready answer, particularly if the answer is turned directly against the PM, your usefulness, on that project at least, would be over.

Consider, too, the consequences in respect of the functional position of the target and his/her relationship with the functional superior. It is advisable to ascertain first whether there would be repercussions up and down the hierarchy. It is often possible and less traumatic to obtain removal of a poorly functioning team member by negotiation with his or her functional manager. In any event, hold your temper in check at all times; be patient and reasonable. If you must resort to confrontation, consider it well beforehand and, above all – be right!

Punctuality

Establish early in the life of the project that punctuality is supremely important. It is a state of mind, a personality trait, but it is something that **should be taught and may be learned**. It is an important asset of the successful project manager. It must be inculcated into all members of the team to the degree possible. Use the attitude towards meetings as a guide to performance. Team members who are late for meetings will probably also be late in performing tasks that are critical elements of the project schedule. If a meeting is scheduled for 10.00 am, the person in the Chair should call the meeting to order **at that precise time.**

Look at punctuality this way. Why should you break a commitment to the next task you are due to perform, or to the person or group you have agreed to meet to accommodate the tardiness of the person or group you are presently dealing with? Keeping in mind the caveat below, it is proper and salutary to terminate a meeting in order to attend a previously arranged appointment.

But, make sure that YOU arrived on time, that you provided all the information required, that you did not permit waffling during the

meeting, that proper records have been kept and that everyone understood, from the beginning, that there was a deadline for the completion of business.

In order to ensure the proper environment for the termination of a meeting at a pre-determined time, you may ask, at commencement, who wishes to speak, for how long, on what subject; then allocate time. If there is insufficient time to cover all the agenda, postpone the less compelling items for a later meeting. Try to avoid arriving at the scheduled end of a meeting with important subjects not addressed otherwise an overrun is inevitable. Start to wind up the meeting soon enough to ensure that minutes have been agreed and noted and that paper shuffling is finished and goodbyes said.

Punctuality is equally important in the conduct of day-to-day business. If you say you will telephone at a certain time, make sure that you do, even if to tell someone that you have nothing to say. Such precision strengthens your dealings with the team and others by reinforcing universal acceptance of punctuality while establishing your own reliability. This in itself is an inducement to others to perform similarly.

> *Employed in the architecture branch of a large builder in the UK while studying part-time, I was asked to work overtime. The money was useful so I stayed the first evening till eight pm. On checking out, there was a book to be signed giving name, finishing time and signature. Of the dozen names ahead of mine, the last four had signed out at ten-thirty pm. I entered the actual time. There was a chill in the drawing office the following week but I was not faced with the same dilemma again. Perhaps a dilemma of ethics rather than punctuality, but truly a different slant on time-keeping.*

Another way of looking at punctuality. Time-keeping is similar to budgeting. Just as many architects or engineers or other specialists *(may they forgive me this allusion)* can design to 10% over the budget but not to the precise budget, so most people can arrive at a meeting ten minutes late but not precisely on time. *I have never been able to understand this and am generally regarded as being a little weird – especially by my wife who subscribes to the belief that parties scheduled for 8:00 pm are expected to start at 9:00 pm!*

> As Contracts Manager on a large design/build project, I made a point
> of keeping the minutes to ensure that the job was done properly. There
> was an official requirement and a real need for a weekly meeting that
> everyone (some twenty people), even the Project Manager, felt too busy
> to attend. Arriving on one occasion, accompanied by two of my own
> staff, we waited 10 minutes, and no-one else having arrived, left the
> meeting room. I wrote the minutes and distributed them to all staff plus
> Head Office and the Client. Under 'attendees', I showed each name with
> present or absent alongside. That made three 'present' and seventeen
> 'absent', including the Chairman. A risky but effective technique!
> Everyone arrived at the next meeting, resentful, irate but on time. The
> Project/Construction Manager never forgave me – you must consider
> how far you want to go.

The project manager has to defeat this syndrome both to save important
project time and to engender an attitude of conscientiousness. You run the
risk of being accused of being pernickety, a nit-picker, unreasonable and
more, but that is the price you pay for being a good project manager. When
example and persuasion fail, there are other ways of achieving your
objective. For an illustration see the previous box.

Punctuality is polite and proper; everyone knows s/he should be on time.
You may never get an overt objection but there will be discontent if you
insist on unequivocal timeliness. So remember; once you establish the
parameters, stick to them yourself – you can never afford to be late. Never.
NEVER.

> In San José, Costa Rica, my wife and I gave an afternoon party to our
> mostly Costa Rican associates. The invitations contained a miniature
> schedule of timed activities such as Arrive, Introductions, Cocktail,
> Conversation, Dine, etc., finishing with 'Depart'. My reputation for
> punctuality already well established, everyone was on time! Not
> unexpectedly, the 'Depart' milestone was postponed. Marco Antonio
> Lopez, an expert engineer and excellent project manager, also displayed
> brilliance on guitar – we all urged him to continue playing and singing.

📖 *'Communication, Meetings, Quorum'*

Quorum

The quorum as a criterion of a meeting is, by extension, an often unfortunate criterion of the effectiveness of the committee meeting itself. As for the large committee, so the larger the quorum, the more difficult to assemble when required and the more difficult to handle. Parsimony in creating a quorum should be as severe as the economy practised in developing a committee and any other group that must, of necessity, meet to advance the implementation of the project.

In other words – keep the committee small and keep the quorum small. If people are really interested in what is going on, they will make the effort to be there. If they know that the quorum is so small that decisions are likely to be made without them, they may find they have a further inducement – other than the advancement of the project and simple good manners – to be at the meeting.

It will not be easy to insist on a small quorum. You will find that each department, each element involved in the project, will wish to be assured by regulation rather than by diligence that they have a say in decisions affecting the project. There has to be a little rationality exercised as well; a quorum of three for a committee of thirty might seem anomalous. Pray that you are never involved in a committee of that magnitude.

📖 *'Communication, Meetings, Quorum'*

3

Responsibility

Accountability determines, functions, relationships and activities

---

General

Responsibility is much misunderstood, not only as a principle but in the application and interpretation of the principle. Responsibility in project management terms, and perhaps in general terms, is not simply what one does, not activity, not role but **accountability** and should be defined exclusively, separately as such. Philosophically, it is sufficient to know to whom and for what one is accountable to determine all one's relationships, functions and activities. Ideally, the application of ethical behaviour, logic and common-sense to the principle of accountability (responsibility) ensures that all else follows.

Obviously it is not that simple or plans of operation, procedures manuals and responsibility charts would not be required. However, if the basic precept is kept in mind, then the logical consequences of responsibility, the practical applications of that responsibility (the 'role') are easier to define.

'Responsibility, Responsibility'; 'Responsibility, Role' and *'Responsibility, Job Description'*

Activity

An activity (doing something) is generated by the requirement to be accountable to someone for something. As mentioned above, the activity is engendered by the application of logic, common-sense and ethical behaviour to this requirement. In project management terms 'activity' is considered more than just doing something but is one of many elements of the project, a whole series of which constitute the project itself.

📖 *'Communication, Language, Definitions'*

Approvals

It is more usual than exceptional for a project manager to be assigned responsibility without adequate authority. In carrying out one's responsibilities, lack of authority, as often as not, creates major difficulties in making a case through a multiplicity of hierarchical levels. You may be forgiven for believing that any number of levels is too many when bending all your efforts to planning or implementing a project and an absence of approvals is delaying the work.

The **consultant** project manager may demand the authority that goes with responsibility as a concomitant of his employment contract. It is more difficult for the **employee** but the ideal should be striven for: that **authority should match responsibility**. If one has the authority, it is much easier to make the right decisions (your own **approvals**) because there is no excuse for making mistakes.

Given the probability that such authority will not be sanctioned, the project manager must protect him or herself by such careful planning and scheduling of approvals that it is made clear to everyone (especially higher authority) that decisions/approvals beyond the authority of the project manager will be required and that they will need to be made promptly. Make it clear, also, exactly who, which individual or group authority will have to make the decisions.

During planning, make sure these requirements are brought to the attention of the authorities and allow plenty of time for those persons to object to the responsibility; if they do so, ask for an alternative. If you can't get a clear ruling, make sure that the situation is well documented; preferably in chart form as shown in *'Planning, Approvals'*.

This need to establish approval requirements is similarly applicable when working directly for a client on a contract basis. The contract performance schedule should clearly indicate approval milestones and show the amount of time available for the client to give approval – which should equally be considered a contractual obligation on the part of the client.

📖 *'Planning, Approvals'*

Attitude

Think back on those occasions when you have discussed your beliefs and ideas with firmness and had your opinion or decision accepted and then contemplate those superficially similar occasions when you have said comparable things but not believed them with the same fervour. Which were the better received?

'Attitude' is something more than a physically-apparent reflection of an inner thought. It is an emanation from the subconscious that can be perceived, sensed by others. If you find this difficult to accept, reflect on the salesman that really believes in his product or merely tries to **persuade** you that he believes in it. If this all sounds a little metaphysical, try it for yourself.

So, when I suggest that the key to successful project management is attitude, I mean more than simply shaping your activities to reflect what the world expects to see; I am referring to a true dedication to the spirit of good project management – the desire to get it right, to suffer the inconveniences necessary to get the job done and the willingness to risk your popularity. It is a question of really believing in what you are doing.

Authority

The matrix organisation is as valuable in its proper application as is functional management and generally is accepted as the norm for most project management. Although team spirit is essential to successful project management and is to be encouraged, no matter how sound the matrix theory, there has to be a leader and there has to be **authority** and it must be available to the project manager by obvious unequivocal delegation in clear unequivocal terms. There are bound to be limitations on that authority but everyone must know what they are; they should be made clear by the plan of operation in both the organisation element and the job descriptions.

The more remote the supreme controlling authority above the project manager in the hierarchical system, the more uncertain the success of the project. The **last word** should be as close to the team leadership as possible.

As the members of a matrix team usually continue to report to a line manager (functional manager), it is essential that the project manager be at a reporting level one above that of the superior of each member of the team. Put another way; the project manager should report to (receive delegated authority from) a superior in the hierarchy at least two echelons above the level of any team member. This gives the project manager effective recourse against a recalcitrant team member when push comes to shove. (It is most often the case that all team members are at roughly the same hierarchical level; if not, if one is more exalted, then diplomacy will have to substitute for authority.)

The establishment of the **moral** authority of the project manager (though the theoretical ideal in the creation of the happy team) is usually painfully time-consuming. In large organisations familiar with project management, the project matrix may be readily accepted, a variation of 'authority' acknowledged and therefore not a problem. More familiarly, the project manager must devote the earlier stages of project development to the exercise of his or her diplomatic skills in persuading the team to follow his or her lead.

This is one of the major trials of a project manager and must be accepted as part of the job where the matrix method has not thoroughly taken hold or where, within the hierarchy, it is even considered ineffective. Given willing cooperation, there is no doubt of the matrix's eventual effectiveness in advancing the project but it can be disconcerting when negative pressure on the team is exerted from middle-level management that has not been convinced of its efficacy.

> ## The project manager rarely has authority to match responsibility

However, when there is a crisis, remember who will be blamed if things go wrong – the project manager; team loyalty forbids blaming team members. So make bold decisions when they are required. Assert the authority necessary; take all the formal, sequential steps in the exertion of that authority; tact first, gentle pressure next, confrontation at a meeting, a pointed reference in the minutes of a meeting, the threat of going over the malefactor's head and, if all this fails, ultimate recourse to the higher authority referred to above. Retain the option of relinquishing your position as a last resort when a question of principle is involved. **But, above all, be sure you are right!**

Control

Control and authority should mean the same thing and do so in the well-organised and firmly-founded project. However, despite what may seem a clear description and delineation of authority in the plan of operation or the procedures manual, it can occur, by error or by omission, that effective control is hidden or simply not recognised. In any project, 'practical' control is in the hands of whomsoever controls the money.

In organisations with an established hierarchy, the word 'control' is sometimes considered the equivalent of a four-letter word but the more control the project manager is allowed the more likely is constructive project completion.

The project manager must **control expenditure** whether or not the team has a cost control expert. It is a requirement of the project manager that his/her training, background and enthusiasms be for careful disbursement of funds and that acquired knowledge be such that valid judgements can be made on the advice received. Relinquishing this authority to a cost control, an accounting element or any other component means surrendering control of the project.

Similarly, an excess of 'approvals' transfers and diffuses control to a variety of levels in a hierarchy. Obviously, there have to be checks and balances against wilful wasting of project funds and higher authority (the client) has ultimate responsibility for expenditure. But where these approvals are required – and they should be as few as permissible – indicate them in the plan of operation by schedule and by magnitude of authority.

At the same time, show clearly the spending limits of the project manger, of all team members and organisations employed by the client in so far as they affect the project. The amount of money one is allowed to disburse and the strictures on that responsibility are an indication of the level of 'control'.

Should a contractor find him/herself required to make disbursement decisions on behalf of the client, the same imperatives apply; make sure there is a stipulation in the contract of the amounts that may be spent without specific approval and what they encompass. This protects both client and the contractor.

📖 *'Communication, Charts & Diagrams – Organigram'; Organisation, Control'; 'Planning, Control'; 'Responsibility, Authority'*

Decisions

Difficult decisions are usually the result of not having made one or more easy decisions or not having made any decision at all. It may seem trite that making a telephone call requires first making a decision but, if the subject matter is likely to be tendentious or the person you are calling to be obstreperous, it is all too easy to delay the call, postpone the unpleasantness, to the eventual detriment of the project. Procrastination for whatever reason and, however minor, spells eventual death for the project.

Consider, too, the many levels of decision-making. All too often a decision that is **not** made at level 1 (in this explanation, the lowest hierarchical level), passes to level 2 where, if not noticed, it is compounded and by the time it reaches level 3 has become a **crisis**. A 'decision' in a design project may be as simple as the drawing of a line or increasing a specification quality standard. A 'decision' in a planning exercise may be the difference between stipulating **requiring** a report and **requesting** a report. Please do not treat this as a triviality. Everything included in a plan or proposal has potential contractual implications. Deciding on the correct word to use may save or lose a project. **Give the question of decision-making at every level its proper importance.**

> ## Make the easy decisions now to avoid having to make the difficult decisions later

It is imperative to have competent staff at all levels making these 'decisions' that are their responsibility and within their capability. Within this responsibility lies the responsibility for cost control as well as for quality and the overall integrity of the project. The technician or professional that is aware of the project budget (as should be the case) and the share for which their department is responsible, has the opportunity on an hourly basis to destroy the project or to save it.

> ## Important decisions are constantly being made at all activity levels

The project manager must ensure that there is a universal awareness of this within the project team and each team member's staff. Failure to do so and to **monitor accuracy and quality at each stage of production** as well as to make the small decisions that engender that quality and accuracy can lead to those difficult decisions that are so much harder to deal with at a later date.

The question of competence at all levels is a difficult one. Adequate supervision (monitoring) and checking of the work as it proceeds is accepted as happening in a normal work environment. It does to a degree. The project manager must ensure that it occurs on his/her project to the standard that will guarantee the proper planning and implementation of the project. Standards must be established and adhered to. It is incumbent on the project manager to ensure that there is sufficient cross-checking between team elements at sufficiently frequent stages to ensure that those low-level errors mentioned are caught before they assume an unwarranted authenticity as they move up through the project structure. Sadly, this is a much-neglected exercise in all management, including project management.

📖 *'Planning, Checking'* and *'Monitoring'* section

Ethics

Accountability
In order to perform most effectively to the benefit of the project, it is essential that the project manager (and all team members) be aware and conscious at all times of what they are responsible for and to whom they are accountable.

Accountability and responsibility are distinct from role, activities or actions, except insofar as the consciousness of responsibility can and will affect them.

In private industry, the **consultant** project manager has little problem. The project manager is responsible, accountable, to the client paying the fee. The only overriding caveat is that the law must not be infringed.

In such a contractual relationship, should there be pressure to perform some illegal or doubtful action, invoke your contract for services, which should contain protection and compensation clauses for such a contingency. If necessary, be prepared to resign on such a point of principle.

Some other examples of project manager (PM) accountability relationships that illustrate the point are:

- an **employee PM in the private sector**
- an **employee PM in government**
- an **employee PM working for a charitable organisation.**

In these examples, the basic ethic is simple enough. In the first case, the responsibility is to the **shareholder**; in the second to the **taxpayer;** and in the third the PM is ultimately accountable to the **donors** who sponsor the charity.

You will probably find that this concept is universally accepted in a philosophical sense but ignored or forgotten in the practical application. There are usually a good many bodies (directors, managers, officers) between the project manager and those to whom one is ultimately accountable; many of them will think the project manager is responsible to them alone, having long since forgotten the source of funds in the satisfaction of spending them.

Give this a lot of thought. There **should** be no conflict between morality and good management. Each project manager must decide for him/herself how far to go in serving the **rightful** client, how much respect to give to conscience and if compromise of principle will not only get the job done but also allow a good night's sleep. Nor would it do any harm to consider as well that unethical behaviour has a nasty propensity for catching up with one later.

The third case is not quite so clear-cut as the others. Charitable organisations also serve a **beneficiary**. The beneficiary is supposedly represented by the donor and this is usually the case. However, there is often a confusion as to what the beneficiary truly needs. The project manager is obligated to interpret this need to the best of his or her ability and to convey the information through the appropriate channels. It may be anticipated that there will sometimes be disagreement between donor (represented by an organisation) and beneficiary but this is a moral issue for the two parties rather than the project manager (PM) and the PM can be expected to do no more than provide the best advice possible.

---

*At a meeting (about 30 people – an unlikely size for useful decision-making, you may think) on a large government project, dining chairs were being considered. The upholstery material was exquisite but totally inappropriate for a cafeteria: the price was extortionate. When asked for my opinion (I was the Contracts Manager), I said **'what would the taxpayer say?'** A stunned silence; twenty-nine pairs of eyes turned towards me. Then they all looked quickly away and the Chairman passed on to my neighbour and asked for more comments.*

Change/improvement

You will constantly encounter or find yourself part of systems, methods and policies that are ineffective, unfair, amoral or merely irritating. It is a mistake to believe that this cannot be changed. (improved). You may not be able to transform it totally but you are entitled, in fact morally required, to chip away at a malevolent structure.

We all can – and should – improve the system

However, if you wish the system and yourself to benefit in fact rather than simply to receive plaudits, it is important not to seek overt personal recognition for any improvement you are fortunate enough to accomplish. Once convinced of the benefit of a change, those in higher authority, with the ultimate capacity to make the transformation, may receive the credit. The wise project manager and the wise employee are satisfied with improved circumstances, conducive to good project management, however they are initiated and whether formally recognised or not.

Client 1
Despite what it says under *'Ethics, Accountability'*, you normally have a professional **and friendly** interaction with the 'client'. Your primary responsibility is to the client as the representative of the providers of funds. You may sometimes find yourself fighting your own organisation for the rights of the client. In a large bureaucratic environment, one of the more certain ways of courting unpopularity is to insist that the client always be served – the client representing either the taxpayer, the shareholder or other source of funds.

    'Responsibility, Ethics, Accountability'

Client 2
The 'client' is always the person or persons or organisation that you are working for **now**. The person who may become a client is still not a client. The significance of this is that one must not jeopardise the interests of the person or company for whom one is working in order to increase one's clientele. Promising, for instance, that a document, a proposal, a design can be produced quickly in order to obtain a contract is not justifiable if it involves neglecting your current workload and delaying work in hand. *The client you have in the hand is worth two in the bush.*
    This is not just an ethical concept. It is in the manager's self interest. Adopting a policy of seizing every opportunity no matter what the consequences will unnecessarily burden your staff and eventually imperil

your relationships with all your clients. The inevitable result of such a working or management methodology is, first, the neglect of one project and , ultimately, the neglect of them all.

> **Do not penalise the client you have by taking on more new work than you can handle**

Error

Always admit to error when you make one (or more). Everyone makes mistakes and it is better to get the acrimony out of the way as soon as possible and get on with the remedial measures. A project manager cannot maintain a respected reputation if the team are all aware that s/he is too pig-headed or unsure to confess to mistakes. You may think that ignoring or not admitting to an error will make others forget. It has the contrary effect – they remember forever.

Also, admit to error by the team and accept personal responsibility for the error. But defend the member responsible, as part of your team, not even naming that person unless absolutely necessary. This is not just a proper morality; it encourages loyalty to the team and stimulates improvement in performance

> *I worked for a manager who built his entire career on cheerfully admitting to error. He was really not very bright but succeeded, by means of an engaging personality, in achieving a position as a Chief Engineer with a multi-national corporation. He blundered constantly but was so ready to admit his mistakes, with such disarming frankness and even with enthusiasm that he was universally admired for his candour and maintained his position for some years. Making willful errors is not recommended as a policy but this example serves to suggest that mistakes confessed are readily forgiven, the confession applauded and the error forgotten.*

Corruption

This may seem a harsh word in a project management context but most dictionary definitions are comparably sweeping; 'corruption' includes the simplest deviation from the correct path to the ultimate debauchery.

Never accept anything, **anything**, from someone who is beholden to you or your organisation for all or part of their income or other benefits. It is important for a project manager to be able to say, honestly, at all times 'I never accepted anything, not even a cup of coffee from anyone.' You may never be required to say this to others but you must always be able to say it to yourself.

This is an ethical concept that is decided between each person and his conscience; it may be thought that 'corruption' is too strong a word for what is described. The advice I give is what I have determined the best method of handling the 'cup-of-coffee, etc.' problem. If you follow it, you may acquire a reputation for eccentricity or worse, for being sanctimonious; an inconvenience, perhaps, but it will not diminish your effectiveness.

> *As Contracts Manager (CM), in order to avoid outright offence in an environment where gifts (bribes?) are common, I accepted a Christmas hamper from a sub-contractor, but donated it to the Salvation Army, making sure I got a receipt. On another occasion, in a consultant inspection position, at Christmas, I reluctantly took a case of scotch from a contractor. Offence avoided, I then wrapped each bottle individually and presented them to the staff of the contractor. The contractor had fulfilled what he thought was his 'obligation' and I had avoided direct offence. Of course, everyone recognised the steps of the 'dance'. But in not enjoying the gifts, not benefiting from them, I consider that I did not compromise myself.*

For myself, I will accept a cup of coffee from a communal coffee pot in an office but not allow anyone to buy me one in a restaurant. This often results in my instituting the expensive defence mechanism of buying all the coffee but it avoids any suggestion of compromise.

You may often hear, as justification for acceptance of a bottle of liquor or other gift, 'No-one believes I can be bought for something so trivial'. No doubt this is true but could that person be bought for three bottles, a case, a brewery? Again, probably not but where does one stop? And what is the **public perception**? Never accept the rationalisation that it is common practice, that everyone does it. Better to avoid the problem altogether – not easy to do but who said being a project manager was easy?.

If all this sounds a little bit far-fetched and even self-righteous (it is difficult), think about the dangers of taking the first step on any road that may lead to **misunderstanding**. What I am talking about is simple common-sense; if you want to stay out of trouble don't allow yourself to be accused of being in someone else's pocket. The fact that it is untrue has nothing to do with the case; just read the newspaper to discover how many people, once tarred by rumour, carry the mark for years. Above all, don't allow yourself to feel embarrassed at the refusal of a proffered gift, be it a cup of coffee or a Cadillac. It is possible to be polite when doing so. Say, for example, 'You are really very kind but my company doesn't allow me to accept even the smallest token.'

Team

All members of the team must feel an equal sense of responsibility for the project. The inculcation of this spirit is one of those difficult things required of the project manager (PM) – one of the PM's key functions. Because errors allowed to occur at the basic levels of project development increase in complexity and impact as they pass, uncorrected, up the ladder of responsibility, so it is more important to avoid error at those levels. Competent workers, imbued with the team spirit, aware that the project success depends as much on them as the project manager, will take that little extra trouble with their work.

> **Motivate and support the team to the ultimate benefit of the project**

An important element in the fostering of this attitude is a requirement of the project manager to support the team at all times. That, without trying to cover up error, the integrity of the team be maintained and the responsibility that is the project manager's be accepted when error does occur, without trying to shift the blame to a subordinate. The buck has a nasty inclination to stop at the project manager as it should with all managers. If a subordinate fouls up, it means that **management** was incompetent, unobservant, badly organised or disinterested.

And, please, there is no such thing as a 'computer error'; they can only tell us what they have already been told. The computer is a tool. If someone cuts off a leg with a saw, it is not referred to as a 'saw error'.

📖 *'Organisation, Project Team'*; *'Responsibility, Decisions'* and *'Responsibility, Ethics, Error'*

Hierarchy 1

It is surprising how often two people in the same organisation or team are shown as having overlapping responsibilities and/or duties. Less surprising, in that it occurs more often, is that some positions are shown as being responsible (reporting to) more than one position in the hierarchy. This is especially true of support staff; for instance, the services of a secretary may be shown as being shared by more than one officer.

This is acceptable if it is handled in a proper manner. A secretary, or any position, must **report** to (take instructions from) only one person and work for others must be agreed with that person in consultation with the secretary.

This is not an attempt to enter into labour relations matters but to ensure good management – an enormous amount of bad feeling is generated and efficiency jeopardised when a person has too many bosses: one is enough! Make sure this error, for error it is, does not occur at **any** reporting level.

📖 *'Communication, Charts'*

Hierarchy 2

In respect of giving instructions, the project manager should always set a good example by passing instructions through the system. Do not attempt to by-pass an established authority or line of authority (including your own subordinates) by giving an order to an employee responsible to that other authority.

If urgency demands a divergence from the proper hierarchical path, make sure you inform the person who has been by-passed at the earliest possible moment and also substantiate the instruction in writing in order to reassure and hold the subordinate safe from recrimination. In doing this, you protect someone else's position which, for the proper project manager, is equally as important as protecting oneself.

Job description (role definition)

In writing job descriptions, always differentiate between 'Responsibility' and 'Role'. Each should be written as a separate element, otherwise confusion may occur. The indispensable element of a job description is the 'responsibility'. If this is clearly stated, the role, actions, activities, etc. follow logically and inevitably. In the same way that the preamble to a law generates rules and regulations, so does 'responsibility' produce a 'role'. In the case of a law, often, very often, the principles of the preamble are forgotten and the regulations seem to become the law. Similarly, a 'role' can seem to be an end in itself when the reality is that responsibility governs role.

This is not to say that, when responsibility is clear, role definition is sufficiently obvious as not to require detailed definition. However, in the best of all possible worlds, one could simply say, for instance, that the Prime Minister is 'responsible for the well-being and welfare of all Her Majesty's subjects' or the President is similarly responsible for his/her citizens. If this were kept in mind and the behaviour of them both accorded with that precept in every matter, there would be no need to describe every activity required to fulfil that requirement. However, theoretical need or not and prime ministers and presidents being human, it is advisable to describe the role (job description) in detail – just to keep them on their toes. This applies equally to project managers and team members.

A typical job description should contain information on, at least, the following items:

- Title
- Reports to (accountable to)
- Instructs
- Liaises with
- Responsibilities
- Activities.

The last item, 'Activities', that sustain and substantiate the responsibilities, may be stipulated under separate headings in respect of differing aspects of role.

Responsibility governs role

An example, taken from the same organisation for which the 'contents' are illustrated under 'Procedures Manual', follows. Because, in this example, the job description is for a committee, more information is required for some aspects of the description than for an individual ('membership' and the constitution of a 'quorum', for instance) and some do not apply except in a somewhat abstruse sense. (NGO means Non-Governmental Organisation)

ROLE DEFINITION   (Job Description)

PROGRAM COMMITTEE   (PC)

REPORTS TO	N/A (independent advisory committee)
INSTRUCTS	N/A (advisory capacity only)
LIAISES	Executing Agency
	Sponsor
	NGO Community

MEMBERSHIP	**Voting Members**
	5 individuals, nominated by registered NGOs
	1 individual, nominated by (an umbrella organisation)
	1 Sponsor Agency representative
	Non-voting Members
	Program Manager of the Program Executing Agency

QUORUM A quorum comprises the Chair or duly appointed Acting Chair, the Sponsor Representative and two other voting members. The Chair or Acting Chair shall have the deciding vote in the event of a tie.

TERM Members shall serve a 2-year term with 3 members being replaced at the end of a 2-year cycle. The Sponsor member will serve as agreed by the Sponsor/NGO. To initiate a rotational system and avoid a large number of members leaving in any one year, 3 members of the initial PC shall serve a 3-year term. Thereafter, all members shall serve 2-year terms. Members are required to attend all PC meetings. In any event, each member shall personally attend a minimum of two meetings. Members who fail to attend 2 consecutive meetings without (in the judgement of the other PC members) sufficient justification shall be assumed to have resigned from the PC and the ExA will be asked to solicit nominations to fill the position.

RESPONSIBILITIES The PC undertakes an advisory responsibility in respect of the disposition of the funds provided for Program projects and in the development of policy for the Program. In carrying out these responsibilities, the PC shall:

ACTIVITIES **1) GENERAL**
Meet as a Committee at least 4 times per calendar year on predetermined dates in order to:
a) review and recommend funding policies such as the standards and criteria for the granting of funds and ensure that these and other Program norms conform to established Sponsor criteria;
b) propose special studies, analyses and reports that will assist the PC to fulfil its mandate;

91

c) make recommendations for training programmes or projects as the Committee may determine necessary from time to time and consider similar proposals either from the Executing Agency (ExA) or the NGO community;

d) review this Procedures Manual from time to time and make recommendations to the ExA for improvements

e) attend an orientation session prior to the commencement of their term, approve in committee and attend any training session organised for the PC by the ExA;

f) notify the ExA if unable to attend a meeting or otherwise unable to fulfil their obligations;

g) participate in Program outreach activities by communicating with NGO colleagues and partners;

h) propose and form sub-committees of the PC as required to study special aspects of the PC responsibilities and activities;

I) participate in programme sub-committees according to their interests and as requested by the ExA or the PC.

j) ensure that all decisions, recommendations and proposals are recorded in the minutes of each meeting and that these minutes are properly distributed to all members of the PC and all other interested parties;

k) in the case of disagreements with the recommendations of the ExA or where a NGO has expressed dissatisfaction with the PC's recommendation, and when the PC member is unable to resolve the matter or decides that it should be reviewed at a higher management level, enter the item in the minutes with a request for review by Sponsor management;

l) when requested or deemed advisable, recommend an institutional review of an NGO within the Program that intends to seek direct financing from the Sponsor, study the proposal and make a recommendation to Sponsor;

2) PROJECTS

a) act as the sole advisory authority in respect of the recommendation of the allocation of matching funds to Program projects proposed to the ExA by the NGO community;

b) receive project proposals from the NGO community after review, analysis and written commentary by the ExA;

c) individual members of the PC shall study and analyse

these proposals prior to a review, discussion and appraisal under Committee conditions;

d) in formal session, determine the conformity of project proposals to the criteria governing approval of matching funds to suitable projects;

e) in respect of all proposals, dispose of them by one of the following alternatives:

- recommend a proposal for matching funding
- recommend a proposal contingent on acceptance of suggested minor modifications to be agreed between the ExA and the proponent
- refer a proposal to the ExA for additional study and recommendations
- for cogent and convincing reasons, postpone review of a proposal to a subsequent meeting
- reject a proposal, giving substantive reasons for the rejection

f) receive acknowledgement from the ExA of acceptance of recommendations and approval of funding;

g) consider, in the same terms as project proposals, proposals for additional monitoring, evaluations, audits, research, training, and counselling either for particular projects or NGOs or for the NGO community, and make recommendations for implementation to the ExA;

h) maintain records of decisions made at all meetings by agreeing the content of the decisions during the meeting and recording these decisions as minutes of the meeting: **the Chair shall be responsible for ensuring this procedure** (the ExA shall provide administrative services);

3) COMMITTEE STRUCTURE

In respect of the constitution of the PC, the Committee shall:

a) at the last meeting of each second calendar year, vote on and appoint a member as Chair for the following two years;

b) instruct the ExA to call for nominations from the NGO community for the replacement of 3 members who have completed their 2-year term as PC Members;

c) as a committee, review proposals for membership, nominate, second and vote on the appointment of new

members;
d) ensure the maintenance by the ExA of an attendance record for members of the PC;
e) as necessary request the ExA to call for nominations from the NGO community to replace members who have resigned or who are deemed to have resigned.

The previous Job Description/Role Definition would be most suitable for certain committees of a Non-Governmental Organisation. It is presented here only to indicate the amount of detail required for an organisation with an on-going commitment to an aid programme that consists of numerous projects each year which are to be implemented by a number of different, independent managers.

> **Mixing 'role' and 'responsibility' facilitates the task of the lazy project manager or planner but confuses those who are later called upon to determine where one ends and the other begins**

📖 *'Responsibility, Responsibility'*

Organigram

An organigram (organisation chart) ties together, while differentiating, the responsibilities of the many components either of an organisation or a project team and its related entities. It also indicates roles to a limited extent and may show other information, including indications of payment routing. It is as useful to the small project as the large and must not be neglected.

📖 *'Communication – Charts/Diagrams'* and *'Planning, Plan of Operation'*

Responsibility and role

Responsibility and role are more often than not written as one subject. They are not the same but are not easy to separate from each other – which may be the reason for their usually being written as one (let's do it the easy way!). However, because the important element, the fundamental element, in this description is that of **responsibility**, it is more useful and appropriate to show it as a distinct element.

Role itself is a product of and depends entirely on responsibility but the role may be different in many cases where the responsibility is similar. When the 'responsibility' is known and clearly described, then the role can more readily be defined within the context of the other parameters governing the position.

For example, the **responsibility** of a project manager on a space probe mission may be described in very similar general terms to those of a project manager building one house. The nature of the **activities** involved in the execution of the work are the parameters determining the **roles** of the two distinct positions and these are **very** different.

📖 *'Responsibility, Job Description'*; *'Responsibility, Role'*

Responsibility/activity matrix

An indispensable aid to the planning and monitoring of a project is the responsibility/activity matrix. It provides valuable information for the development of the organigram, job description, monitoring schedule, contracts, costs, work breakdown structure; in fact, all the tools of project management are enhanced by this invaluable chart.

This is another tool that is as important to the small as the large operator. A building contractor could define all his/her sub-contracts by developing this matrix to correspond to all the trade elements of the construction while assigning a trade contractor to each. Most contractors already do this (perhaps by another name). What is important is to realise that this is a method of assigning **responsibility**; and also the allocation of the principal contractor's responsibilities, so revealing what may otherwise fall between the cracks – ordering of materials to be installed by others, for instance.

There is no consequential difference between the application of this principle to a construction contract, a procurement project, a computer program design, architecture, whatever you will. Putting it on paper in a tabular format provides the project manager and the team with a framework that can be added to, shuffled around as the project progresses. The design of the matrix is essentially a team operation.

Because most organisations operate subsequent projects in similar environments, the first matrix may provide a permanent format for later projects. A bare-bones example for a large overseas project is produced on the next page.

The project manager (PM) is **responsible** for the preparation of the plan of operation (POP). The PM will not, necessarily, prepare it; development of the POP is an 'activity' or, depending on its magnitude, may be considered a 'task'. That particular activity or task may be broken down further into half a dozen or more smaller activities and any or all of the team members might be involved, usually more than are shown in the sample chart that follows.

ARGENTINA PAMPAS WHEAT PROGRAM
Responsibility/Activity Matrix

ACTIVITY	PM	AG.ADV	MIN.AG	FIELD AGENT	CLIENT	PROC'T AGENT	OTHER
Prepare plan of operation	■	○					
Develop budget	■	○		○		○	
Coordination	■	○		○		○	
Training plan	○	■					
Equipment schedule	○	■					
Procurement	○					■	
Shipping	○					■	
Field implementation				■			
Monitor/inspect	■	○					
Approvals			○		■		
Evaluation					■		

■ Prime responsibility
○ Related activity

The responsibility/activity matrix may comprise scores or hundreds of activities. Its complexity is most probably a result of the magnitude of the project. The thoroughness required depends on the stage of planning development and the ultimate requirement for detail. It should be constantly added to and or modified as planning develops and detail should increase correspondingly. Here, a computer will save enormous amounts of time – in fact make the accurate completion of the task possible and maintain it in a current state.

However, even for a small project, this matrix should not be skimped or ignored at any stage as it is a valuable adjunct to contract preparation, project production (implementation), scheduling, preparation of job descriptions, reporting procedures and reporting schedules. It can also facilitate the rational development of the organisation chart (organigram) according to needs, as indicated by the matrix, **not** according to the availability of personnel – frequently the case. (See *'Role'* below)

The activities need not be in order of execution but the closer they are to that order, the more assistance will the matrix provide in the development of the implementation schedule and the easier to master the logic of project development.

Obviously, the project manager is involved in all activities but a careful analysis must be made to avoid complicating the chart unnecessarily by showing his or her every peripheral activity. Experience will teach where to draw the line.

Role

It should not be necessary for this to be said but there is enough evidence that the problem exists to make the caveat necessary. **Never develop an organisation (project or functional) solely in accordance with the availability of personnel.** Commence with the ideal organisation. Then study the hierarchical, organisational and contractual structure. Often it will be found that some contractual or inter-relational concepts have to be reconsidered (to ensure, for instance, that **control** remains where it should be).

Once this is done, review the available personnel. If the complexity of the project requires it and the budget permits, make arrangements to acquire the missing elements. Where this is not possible, consider assigning team members to different (additional) functions within the organisation. **Make sure that such personnel have the capacity to accept a differing degree of responsibility where this applies.** A team member may be an authority in one field but be required to accept a very secondary role in another assigned function If unprepared to do this, that person may become a disruptive influence.

If you are obliged (by circumstances or by higher authority) to accept what you consider unsuitable personnel, do your best to assist them in performing their duties. But also make sure that your misgivings are recorded before accepting the person on the team.

📖 *'Responsibility, Job Description'* ; *'Responsibility, Responsibility'* and *'Organisation, Aptitude'*

Role definition

'Role Definition' is simply a slightly more sophisticated or politically correct way of saying 'Job Description'. I try to avoid political correctness but confess to having used the term myself; perhaps it is more precise in that 'job' has other connotations in some technical and professional fields.

📖 *'Responsibility, Job Description'*

THE RULES OF BUREAUCRACY

Anthony Jay, co-author with Jonathon Lynn, of *Yes, Minister*, in an article for the *London Weekly Telegraph*, identified 10 principal rules of bureaucratic survival. Here I paraphrase six of them as illustrations of what not to do as a project manager.

- **Spread responsibility**. Wrong decisions should be made by more than one person.
- **Keep it a secret**. If people don't know what you are doing, they don't know what you are doing wrong.
- **Avoid risk**. The rewards for success are immeasurably smaller than the penalties for failure.
- **Avoid changes, innovation and hurry.** Maintain the protection of precedent.
- **Avoid measurable standards**. There will be no proof that you have failed.
- **Put all duties and responsibilities on to others**. Never let the buck stop here.

He continues, saying, 'What we discovered while writing *Yes Minister* was that bureaucracies are not passive instruments. They actively create their own agenda. The contrast between party manifesto commitments and the Bills that finally come before the Commons represent the triumph of ministry policy over Ministers' policy.'

This problem of the subversion of policy is a matter of scale. As a project manager, you may well be able to manipulate client policy to suit your agenda. While you are doing this, members of your team may be doing the same thing to you. The lesson is that goals and purposes must be clear and that monitoring must be detailed and consistent at all levels. A client or potential client must be on guard to ensure that the project is designed to meet his, her or, its specific needs.

Please consider this carefully. I have always been astounded in my own work, and at my level of authority, at the amount of influence I could have on a client's project, particularly during the planning stage. I would appreciate your assuming that I always used that influence to the benefit of the project.

4

Communication

Free flow of information is
the essence of good
project management

General

Although everything in this book applies to project management in its broadest application (and most of it to functional or generic management as well), in order to provide a convenient reference point from which to relate the principles, I base most of the conclusions on an assumption of the adoption, by the enterprise or organisation, or the application of matrix management methods for a project in a functional management environment.

Even the smallest project management matrix has a number of technical elements operating semi-independently in their own specialised environment at various levels of expertise. The information these elements produce, the actions they take, affect the project to a greater or lesser degree at differing times in the life of the project.

But at any time an uncommunicated action or developed piece of information can be vital to one or several elements of the team and to related external elements. Failure to communicate such information can be potentially disastrous to the success of the project. Clearly, everyone engaged on the project must be made constantly aware of not only what has been done but what is **being done** and what is anticipated **to be done** – as well as what has **not been done**. This last one may well be the most critical.

Information must be useful

The plan of operation will provide the context for project development and implementation. Within that context, it is for the project manager to ensure that information is transmitted as it is produced, both upward, downward and laterally, at a frequency and in a format sufficient to keep the project moving but without snowing everyone under.

In fact, the true substance of good project management is effective communication through all phases of a project, through feasibility, planning, implementation and evaluation; between all members of the team, at all levels, and those affected by the development of the project. 'Effective' in this case means communicating in a timely manner that cannot be ignored, that will give clear parameters of time and content, can guarantee a response and provide a record; the permanent record is important. There is, of course, the hazard that by following those parameters an error also will be effectively communicated and rapidly implemented. But at least if the origin and nature of the error are fully recorded, there is a starting point for correction.

As with all aspects of project management, there is a line to be drawn. 'Communication' is not just the disseminating of any and all information. Information must be useful. The project environment will have some influence on where the line is drawn between 'useful' and 'what, more paper?' It may be necessary to put more into the record where some of those involved in the project are less than enthusiastic about accepting their due responsibilities. Some of the key elements of communication follow, not necessarily in order of importance.

Action sheet

This is what the name implies; it lists actions required and, to make sure they happen, includes a date and a responsible person (a person, repeat, a person).

It may have any format you prefer: I use the example shown below on an 8½ x 11 inch (or A4) sheet of paper – or several sheets. It can be used as an instruction sheet or can serve as a format for the minutes of meetings. The restricted space and the columnar style tend to impose brevity on the originator. This is always beneficial – anything that reduces paper is beneficial; and any methodology that tends to a tabular format is also beneficial because it makes the writer think and helps the reader comprehend more easily.

ACTION SHEET	Project Title: Project No: Attendees:	Meeting No: Date: Notes by: Purpose:	**Action**		
Item	Proposition/condition		Resolution	By	Date

An **action sheet** may be the record of the decisions of a meeting with arguments recorded briefly in the column 'proposition/condition'. As mentioned above, I use it to record the minutes of a meeting. In project management, especially fast-track projects where days and hours saved are important, it is far more useful than traditional minutes. It eliminates the need to sort through wordy narrative prose to determine the end results. The initials of the responsible person go in the column 'by'. You may find some resistance to such rigidity. The action sheet may be hand written – but legibly.

📖 *'Communication, Meetings, Minutes'*

Annotations

It is often convenient and justifiable to annotate letters, documents, drawings, reports, etc. as a method of communication. However, in order to authenticate the annotation, it is essential to append the date and one's initials.

It is, at the very minimum, irritating and frustrating to find a note of unknown or doubtful origin against an important issue that may already have been resolved or superseded by subsequent events and, because **an unauthenticated annotation has no validity** (try telling that to your boss!), the pursuit of the true status of the issue in these circumstances will almost certainly be very time-consuming and cause actual delay to the project. What is more, and unfortunate, is that such annotations invariably assume an authority they do not merit (with possible contract implications) and have to be either validated or killed.

Any note not properly substantiated in this way should be mentioned as an issue at a team meeting for resolution and inclusion in the minutes. This not only ensures that the information is confirmed and recorded (or eliminated altogether) but, when circumstances demand, can also comprise an act of censure against the perpetrator and indicate a policy for the future.

> **Communication is a two-way street.**
> **The project manager sets and maintains the standard**

In a fast-moving project, if it is agreed that annotations are an acceptable method of communication, then it would not be exaggerating to note the time of day when the annotation is made. These strictures apply equally to a project manager as to a team member. Being in charge is not a licence to flout the essentials of good communication. Better to annotate in ink, too. Illegible, scribbled annotations, whether justified or not in content, are useless if they cannot be read and devalue the thought and enterprise that inspired them. Make sure that you are **communicating** and not simply 'expressing' yourself or blowing off steam. *(If you consider it important to speak clearly to be understood, then it is equally important to write clearly!)*

Never assume that such an annotation can be ignored. When things go wrong at a later date, the note may suddenly acquire a pivotal importance.

📖 *'Communication, Email'; 'Communication, Mail'; 'Communication, Marginal Notes'*

Clarity

In discussions (face-to-face or by telephone), if it seems the interlocutor does not understand, ask questions until the matter is clear. At the risk of causing irritation by seeming to imply that the other party is dense, if you still doubt that the message has been understood, ask some more questions. All too often two people leave a meeting or terminate a telephone call with different ideas of what has been agreed. Where the project manager is involved, he or she is responsible to ensure that this does not happen. This is a buck that cannot be passed. And **follow up with a written confirmation.** *This is another little exercise that may drive people up the wall but you cannot just **assume** that the other person understands or, alternatively, that you have communicated adequately.*

📖 *'Communication, Language'; 'Communication, Meetings'*

Charts and diagrams

Perhaps it is not surprising that many people (more often clients or non-technical personnel) have great difficulty in reading a chart or diagram. This may be because verbal communication is familiar to us all and a chart, because it abruptly presents a great deal of information in a very small physical and time space, initially may seem confusing, perhaps even overwhelming.

A little persuasion and indoctrination soon familiarises people with the essentials of graphic communication and most accept it willingly, even enthusiastically, when fully familiar with the principles. The universal employment of computers and their capacity for ever more aesthetic presentation is making communication by charts and graphics more commonly accepted. Nevertheless the concept is not yet fully appreciated or comprehended.

When viewing a chart or diagram for the first time, take as much time as you need to study it before arriving at a conclusion either as to its intent or its validity. Usually, the person showing it has either had a hand in its creation and understands its implications or has had the opportunity to become familiar with it. Don't allow yourself to be hurried; ask as many questions as are required to make the chart clear. After all, it could be wrong and the written material that would replace it might take hours to read. You are entitled to study it thoroughly and to question what is not instantly clear.

The benefits of charts and diagrams are enormous. Everyone knows, for instance, that a one-sheet organisation chart (organigram) can contain as much information as many sheets of job descriptions. On a chart, total interaction between two people may be indicated by a few words and one line with an arrowhead, whereas the equivalent description of authority flow and reporting requirements by purely verbal means would require several lengthy written paragraphs, maybe several pages; and probably also be confusing.

For the person preparing it, the act of drawing the chart, facilitates the rationalisation of relationships; if a box contains a name and it is connected to another by a line with an arrowhead, we know that the entity at the tail end of the arrow instructs the entity at the arrowhead. A simple concept but one that has critical implications for job descriptions and contracts.

All sorts of concepts may be presented graphically; organisation, information flow, responsibility, contractual relationships, reporting, comparisons of systems, time schedule, procedures and even abstractions – to mention a few.

Organigram

General

The **organigram** (organisation chart) defines many useful concepts immediately and concisely. The four we shall deal with principally are:

- responsibility
- control
- reporting
- contractual relationships

The basic parameters for the organigram are:

- spatial location on the chart does not indicate a hierarchical relationship;
- degree of sophistication is limited only by the amount of information that may (without risking confusion) be squeezed onto the paper;
- there are three common relationships indicated in the charts that follow:

(Note that 'agreement' or 'contract' always has two arrowheads; that the 'control' line only goes in one direction, and 'information/liaison' can pass in one direction or have a reciprocal function)

Other types of lines, including colours and varying thicknesses, may be used for both these and for special functions as you will see in some examples but these are the lines used to express the basic concepts in this manual. Given the sophistication of current software all sorts of complexities can be introduced but the basic principles must be understood and applied.

Because location of an element on the chart is immaterial and because it is vital to indicate control, the arrowheads are essential. **If an arrowhead cannot be indicated, then the relationship is not feasible**; in fact, there is no **logical** relationship unless it is assumed that the line connects two entities of an equal importance – and that seems pretty pointless.

> *In case the reader thinks I am being overly fastidious about this arrowhead detail, a case in point. I saw an organisation chart, widely circulated in a government department, that had no arrowheads but which carried the note that 'position on the chart does not indicate a hierarchical relationship'; leaving open the possibility that the secretary could be instructing the manager. Not a rational possibility, true, but every other relationship was equally questionable; such a chart should be a definitive illustration of legal and organisational relationships. If this doesn't bother you as much as it does me, then perhaps you should not be reading this book.*

Information/liaison lines may lead into the project manager box (or into any other controlled position from a non-controlled entity outside the immediate organisation). Where there are unusual requirements in a project, it is often useful to indicate the nature of the information/liaison relationship as shown here.

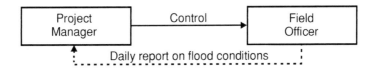

In this example, although the requirement to report is inherent in the control relationship by the Project Manager of the Field Officer (a control line imposes a reverse reporting procedure), the special requirement is reinforced by appearing in the chart in an inescapable manner.

Control

Because organigrams are really about control, contractual relationships (in their broadest sense) and about money, one major organisational principle rules their creation. This is, in three parts.

- Control of money equals control of project; money control is regulated by a contract/agreement or an established hierarchical relationship. Ergo, whoever controls the money, controls the contract and so controls the project.

- Because money control and contract control are synonymous, if you can't withhold payment you have no control of the contract/project.

- There is no moral obligation in a contract; if is not written, referred to or established in law, then it does not apply. So, if you want something to happen, it must be written – or drawn.

The organigram and, consequently, the control system must reflect these concepts. This applies equally to a project that has no outside elements (when all are employees of the same company or organisation) as one with multiple-company interactions. The control of funds rules the progress of the project; for instance, if an *approval*, rather than a *recommendation*, is required by a financial advisor within the company before a disbursement can be made, the control passes to the financial advisor. Should the approval be withheld indefinitely, then the project would stop. This is not likely to happen but delay may occur to a degree sufficient to jeopardise the project.

I agree that total stoppage is not probable but do not take this factor lightly; the question of delay due to tardy approvals or recommendations within the project hierarchy is not just a theoretical concept but a major project management peril.

I have seen a construction project controlled over the head of the project manager by the quantity surveyor/estimator (Q.S.) because he was given the authority to rule on every aspect of cost control; another aspect of the same problem. In this particular case, frequent delays were caused by objections to prices negotiated by the project manager, by requirements to re-measure work by sub-contractors, to perform work studies for particular operations and many others.

All these circumstances were perfectly justifiable – bad faith is not imputed; but the project manager was not allowed to override the decisions and requirements of the Q.S. The manager did not control the project. *Any Q.S. reading this will probably argue that that is the way it should be!*

Keep in mind that **approvals mean control**. When planning the project, make sure that these approvals only occur at the proper levels and that they are kept to a minimum. Spend as much time as is required to convince the client of the requirement for the absolute minimum of approvals. (The 'client' may be, and often is, a superior in the same organisation.)

In many long-established hierarchies, officials are sometimes included in the approval process because they are there, because they have always done it or because we don't want to offend 'old Fred', nor, to be totally politically correct, 'old Phyllis'. Even being downright objectionable may fail to cut them out of the process but it is for the project manager, during the planning process, to show that only absolutely necessary approvals are good approvals.

If a **recommendation** only is required, then there is only a delay factor involved – not a control factor. After trying persuasion, tact and diplomacy, the project manager may resort to overruling a recommendation – at whatever risk to his/her own position.

However a delay outside the control of the project manager may be fatal to the project, so caution is advised when writing the plan of operation (POP) that there be a fall-back position in the event that a recommendation (or an approval) be refused or unreasonably delayed. However, there is often an imposed requirement for a recommendation from the higher levels of authority (the client).

Recommendations and approvals are not the same thing

Where feasible, a provision should be made in the POP for skirting the potential delay or for beginning a new sequence of activities that will advance other elements of the project during the delay period. This can be a tricky exercise and should be approached and implemented with great caution. Study all the potential impacts down the line before deciding that redeployment is better than delay.

📖 *'Planning, Approvals'*

The chart opposite is a minimal organigram (organisation chart) illustrating the use of the various line types.

Although the chart is not designed specifically to expose the conflict condition described below, it is worth following a probable dispute process through the chart to make its implications clear.

In this example, should the site representative (of the Designer), through monitoring activities, discover an error in implementation, s/he may bring it to the attention of the Supervisor with whom there is a liaison relationship. However, because this is only an 'information/liaison' relationship, the sole legal and/or contractual recourse of the site representative in the event of disagreement is to refer the matter back to the Designer.

The Designer, in turn, may discuss the matter with the Project Manager (another liaison/information relationship). But should no resolution be determined, then, for the same reason, the designer must refer back to the Client who would resolve the dispute through the terms of the contract.

ORGANIGRAM

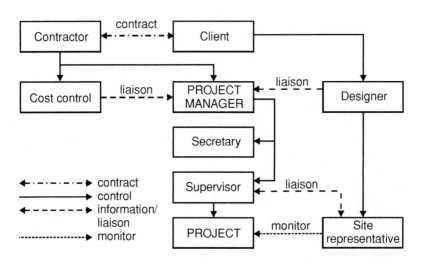

In general, although the contract is an agreement between two equal parties, the client has the edge because the client controls the money – at least on the day when the contract is signed.

It follows that the client should try to maintain this condition (control of the money) because the client who overpays at any time during the life of the contract immediately loses absolute CONTROL at that point.

There is an enormous psychological (and financial) advantage to the contractor who can induce the client to pay beyond the value of work completed. At that point, the client, being fully aware of the circumstance (though this is not necessarily so), would feel inclined to view contractor demands more generously in the hope of inducing the contractor to continue the work so that payments might eventually equal work completed.

For which reason, when the weight of inherent leverage is on the side of the client (a government department, for example) there is often a contractual requirement imposed by the client that, when agreement cannot be reached on the value of the disputed item, the work must be performed without immediate recourse solely on the strength of a written instruction.

This can be very onerous, of course, and invariably leads to wrangling at the completion of the contract; but it is usually accepted by the contractor because of the other benefits of a contract with a government or large corporation. This sheds light on the increase in recent years of consultancies devoted entirely to the rationalisation and negotiation of claims.

Returning to the basics of chart design; various related entities may be grouped in smaller boxes within a larger box to show a general relationship of, for example, department to department, contractor to designer, two unrelated entities that have a general contact/liaison or simply to avoid a multitude of lines from a manager to a number of subordinates. An example follows.

ORGANIGRAM

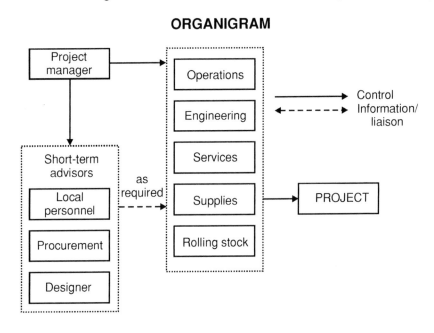

Note in the previous example that the project manager controls all the short-term advisors. Normally the project manager's job description should permit the deputisation of any of the full-time personnel (Operations, Engineering, Services, Supplies, Rolling Stock) to direct (**control**) the short-term advisors.

Alternatives

Simple organigrams can be used quickly to clarify alternative management methods in order to aid a decision on which is the better. The following two charts show two management methodologies for implementation of an overseas project. The first is by a consortium of architects, engineers and construction managers contracting joint services to a client.

MANAGEMENT BY CONSORTIUM

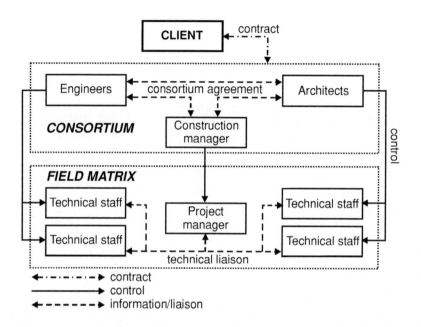

The weakness of this first methodology (the consortium) is illustrated by the interrelationship of the field staff (being strictly a liaison condition), the field staff being dependent in their activities and liaison on the consortium agreement between the Engineers, Architects and Construction Managers. The authority of each professional element in the field is limited by the pressures on and the special interests of its superiors in the consortium.

For effective execution of the project, the 'Project Manager' really needs to have total authority over all technical field staff but, in this case, only has a liaison relationship. He or she cannot have a control relationship because control of each branch of field staff is exercised from within the consortium by the responsible professional.

The chart graphically and immediately indicates this weakness in that three control lines, from the consortium to the field, return to three separate entities in the consortium; because a control relationship mandates a consequent reverse reporting relationship, it creates a situation *(three probably unrelated reports or, at the best, three different viewpoints!)* that can only confuse head office and delay coordination in the field.

The client is dependent on the goodwill that exists between the partners and on the comprehensiveness of the consortium agreement. Anyone who has worked in construction knows that the relationship between contractors, architects and engineers is a weak reed to lean on in the event of things going wrong. This probably applies equally to any other consortium arrangement. The client will, of course, have reviewed and approved the consortium agreement but, in all probability, has not considered the problems of personality and rivalry that can sabotage such an accord.

Remember that the fact of this being an example in construction practice has nothing to do with the principle. The inherent weakness is in the nature of a consortium itself. The reason that some consortiums (consortia?) occasionally work is that one partner, by reason of personality or knowledge or sheer effrontery, usually dominates the others. Of course, projects usually finish one way or the other in one condition or another, so many institutional clients are prepared to either accept the inconveniences of the consortium or hope that 'this time it will be different'. In the case of a government department, the taxpayer foots the bill for any cost overruns. In all too many instances nobody at the top even appreciates that there was a management problem. You may be sure that project failure will be ascribed to whatever suits the person seeking the justification.

It might be argued that a well-written agreement between the partners of the consortium would resolve this problem – perhaps by two of the partners acknowledging the primacy of the third in matters of field implementation. Theoretically, this is possible but, in real life, it is rarely agreed to initially and if it is, is usually breached in practice. So why would some clients select a consortium in preference to any other management method? The answer may be seen in the next illustration of management by an executing agency. The following chart is for the same project, the client employing an executing agency with full responsibility for selecting and employing whatever professional and technical expertise is required.

The alternative of the employment of an executing agency (ExA) which provides a Project Director (PD) from staff resolves the problem of control. From the chart opposite, it can be seen that the Project Director reports to a position two levels above that of the staff he or she directs. Although the PD may or may not be provided direct authority over other field staff (a liaison line is shown), the control, the moral authority (even in a liaison relationship), is obvious. Recourse of Technical Staff in any dispute with the Project Director is through the sub-consultant to the Executing Agency **which directly controls the Project Director.**

MANAGEMENT BY AN EXECUTING AGENCY

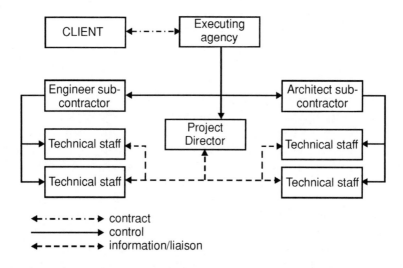

contract	◄ ·─ ·─ ·─ ►
control	─────►
information/liaison	◄ ─ ─ ─ ─ ─ ►

> **Project management by consortium is a contradiction in philosophical and practical terms**

In the example, the terms of reference of the Project Director (and other field staff) should make it clear that any instruction or advice of the PD is authorised by the Executing Agency which controls both professional sub-consultants. Technical staff that perceive an error are at liberty to report back through their line command to the ExA: resolution of the matter is by the ExA without the legal or contractual requirement of reference to any equal partners. It is, of course, understood that the professionals contracted to or employed by the ExA will perform their work within the norms of their profession. The ExA is, by contract with the client, required to provide a proper professional service and will be obliged to listen to any matters raised by those professionals that suggest a deviation from good practice.

The point that must not be overlooked is that the ExA carries **total responsibility** for the success of the project, including a guarantee of the professional quality of the work of the architects and engineers. The client has recourse only against the ExA. It is often the case, with management by executing agency, that the client be allowed a final say in the choice of professionals by the ExA. Of course, by so doing and accepting some part of the responsibility for choice, the client weakens the options for recourse against the ExA in the case of an error by the chosen professionals.

One of the reasons for the unpopularity of the executing agency methodology in construction projects is that, because of the nature of construction, the executing agency is normally a general contractor with a reputation for 'getting things done'. On the other hand, the engineer and architect are seen as being more concerned with their professional reputations and the integrity of the finished product.

I do not care to suggest that contractors are not equally concerned but, historically, the expression of the two theoretically similar points of view has sometimes resulted in either a modestly or substantially different physical manifestation. The principle applies equally with other professionals and in other types of projects. Professional jealousies and conflicts exist throughout every industry. Putting control in the hands of one is bound to upset some of the others – but it is more likely to get the project properly completed

From the point of view of the client, another reason for **not** choosing an executing agency is that control is more obvious and more positive with an executing agency. Decisions, when required, can clearly be seen to be made or not made. There is no attenuation of responsibility through a plethora of consultants each bearing similar responsibility. The client makes a decision and the ExA immediately carries it out. Believe it or not, this is often seen by some as a frightening concept in its immediacy, irreversibility and potential for unequivocal assignment of accountability – and particularly so in the operations of a bureaucratic structure. Don't dismiss this theory as far-fetched – a lot of executives are more concerned with their security, their position, their authority, than with getting the job done.

Finance and procurement

An example of the help that can be provided by an organigram in developing organisation and financial control is shown in the chart that follows. Be patient as you read it and follow the chart. It really does make sense.

AN OVERSEAS AID PROJECT

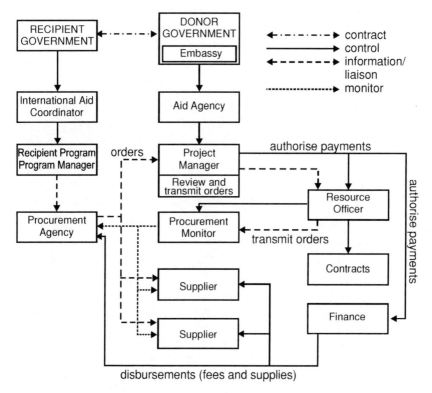

The essence of the information that may be adduced from this chart is:

● **Agreement**

By the agreement between the two governments, funds are authorised to be disbursed for certain programmes or projects. The conditions of the agreement are general; for instance, a sum is assigned for the procurement of agricultural equipment: the specific requirements are designed by the Program Manager of the Recipient Program. The nature of a control line demands reverse reporting, so that the International Aid Coordinator is constantly aware of the overall requirements and will feed this information back to the Recipient Government and so back to the Donor Government by reason of the inter-governmental agreement.

At the same time, the more detailed work of actual procurement is being carried out by the Recipient Program (Program Manager) and more precise data are fed back to the Donor Government Project Manager (PM) from the Procurement Agency upward.

- **Procurement**

  Procurement is by the Recipient Government acting through the state Agency (International Aid Coordinator) which distributes credits to programmes designed to re-build the economy.

  The Program Manager (in effect, the Recipient Project Manager) orders supplies through a nominated Procurement Agency selected from names proposed by the Government originating the aid funds.

  The Procurement Agency consolidates the orders, calls tenders from suppliers, supervises the ordering process and arranges delivery to the Recipient Program. All these operations are advised by copy to the Project Manager.

- **Payment**

  The Procurement Agency confirms all orders to the Project Manager. Because there is liaison at Government level (a required condition of the Loan Agreement), the Project Manager will also constantly be aware of the overall requirements of the Recipient Program.

  Acting through his/her Resource Officer, the PM will verify that the detailed requirement is valid. Assuming that it is, the PM will confirm, through the Finance Department, that payment is to be made to the Supplier and that the Procurement Agency shall receive its fee instalment. The simple existence of the payment (control) line indicates control of the Procurement Agency by the Donor Government. This is the reality of 'whoever controls the money, controls the contract, controls the project.'

- **Monitoring**

  When the Resource Officer confirms the validity of the order to the PM, s/he will at the same time, inform the Procurement Monitor who is charged with monitoring the effectiveness and accuracy of operations by both the Procurement Agency and the Supplier.

From this chart, it is obvious that:

1. agreements are required between:

- the two Governments
- the Recipient Program and the Procurement Agency or Agencies
- the Procurement Agency and the Supplier(s), possibly through a third party (a Donor-Government Agency)
- the Donor Government and the Procurement Monitor.

2. the Resource Officer has an insight into and a review of all contracts through the Contracts Department

3 the Project Manager controls all disbursements through the Finance Department and therefore controls the project on behalf of his client, the Donor Government.

It is also clear that the Agreement between the two governments must include all these anticipated provisions. So the plan of operation (POP) should be written **before** the Agreement or should at least be well advanced, sufficient to identify all the participants with an outline description of their responsibilities and activities when the Agreement is signed.

To fail to prepare the POP in a timely manner risks the omission of vital points from the Agreement and increases the difficulties of writing proper contracts. It is a formula for failure to a greater or lesser degree.

You will see that neither the Project Manager nor his/her Resource Officer has direct contact with either of the Suppliers: there is an arm's-length relationship with the Procurement Monitor serving as monitoring intermediary. The importance of proper selection of this monitor and the necessity of an unequivocal and enforceable contract cannot be over-estimated.

Logical framework analysis

The logical framework analysis (LFA) chart provides an abundance of basic project information for the development of budgets, relationships and tasks. It is essentially a 'planning' tool and is covered in that section. However, it also may serve usefully as a confirmation of requirements for essential channels of communication that must be accounted for, especially in the column 'Means of Verification', wherein sources of information or documentation are shown.

📖 *'Planning, Logical Framework Analysis'*; *'Appendix, LFA'*

Procedures

Complex procedures may usually be clarified by setting them out in graphic form. As an example of the use of a chart/diagram to outline and clarify a procedure, the following chart shows all those activities required to terminate a project in order to justify and authorise final payment. It applies in this case to a construction project but the principle may be applied to most different types of project. There is a great deal of information on the chart but the display of the sequence of operations and the identification of the participants simplifies it to a degree that is hardly possible with a narrative presentation.

The chart was developed for a complex design/build construction project in which there were many (some 85, both large and small) construction contract packages both beginning and terminating sequentially. Such complexity is infrequent but a chart or diagram for the termination procedures of all projects, even the simplest, is strongly recommended. Today, it may be fed into a computer but, for the small operator with multiple projects of the same type, a simple sheet such as that shown may be produced as a standard document for all similar projects. The 'Certificate' referred to is a 'Certificate of Completion' and, in construction projects, is required before final payment may be made.

*The chart opposite is different from those previous in that the **procedures** dominate the activity flow rather than the contributors. The procedures required to complete the contract are the headings of each block of activities (e.g. 'Back-charges' which are claims by the Client against individual contractors). The activities that govern the procedures proceed from box to box, following the arrows. Departments and individuals occupy the boxes wherein those activities are registered. Nevertheless, it is comparatively easy for those individuals to trace their activities through the chart and to determine at what point they are involved and what action is required of them. The departments and individuals involved in this procedure include: Change Control; Area Supervisors; Senior Area Supervisor; Safety Officer; Contractor; Assistant Superintendent; Accounts; Estimator; Drawing Control; Insurance Broker; Design Group; Electrical- Mechanical (E/M); Director of Construction; Contracts Manager, Client, etc.*

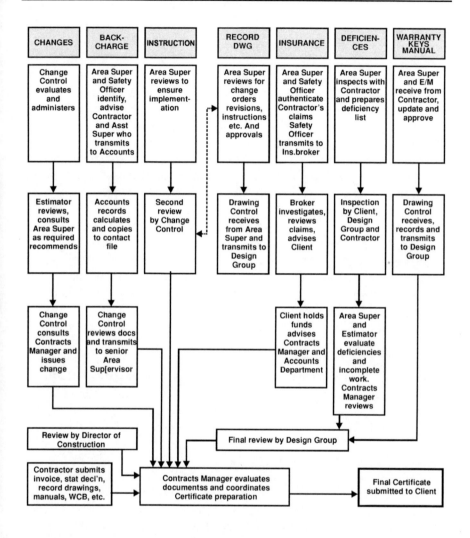

This chart could not and should not completely replace the project procedures manual. Given that the information it contains was set out elsewhere in detail where reference required, the chart provided a quick check to ensure that all activities were being performed in the proper order – and it was a lot easier to read.

Computer

There are thousands of computer programs that facilitate the generation, control and transfer of information. They are an important communication as well as a control tool. But they must be used wisely. To apply a complex computerised system to an inadequate plan is a waste of time. Either the computer program must fit the project plan or the project plan must fit the computer program.. Compatibility in design and scope is essential.

Even though you may not intend to computerise your operations totally, it is often helpful to use a computer program as a guide to project planning; to determine, for instance, by illustrating relationships and sequences of operations, that certain reports and how many reports need to be generated. But, although the program will establish some basic parameters; the content of the report, its frequency and who needs to receive it are generally matters that must be determined by the project team and confirmed by the project manager. I do not doubt that I am treading dangerous ground here. There are certain types of projects (material procurement may be one) that lend themselves to precision of procedures, generating quantities and milestones as an inevitable consequence of the basic procedure. If a computer will do everything for you, by all means use it to the extent possible. But do not be overawed by technology: it is only as useful as those who use it are in control of it. Successful project management was around long before the computer.

It must be said, though, that sophisticated project programmes with multiple projects, fast-track requirements, frequent disbursement deadlines, strict cost-control parameters and multiple resourcing requirements can probably only be handled in a tight time-frame by the use of computer technology. The middle-level manager will probably not be in a position to make a decision in regard to the use of the computer or the software to be employed and will be happy to take advantage of all the facilities offered. Just keep an eye on the other aspects of project management. Do not let the need to feed the computer keep you from **managing** the project.

However, the gradual conversion to computer technology, the tendency of the disk or drive to replace the sheet of paper, also has the potential to change, for instance, the nature of contractual relationships (and the way they are managed), payment procedures and other project management processes. It may not all be to the betterment of project control.

As an example, automated money transfers will expedite payment procedures but have the capacity for making it so automatic that the volume of administrative work per person may be increased to such an extent that the monitoring and evaluation that should precede a payment may be neglected. One could posit that greater facility in administration implies a reduction in cost for that element while disproportionately increasing the cost of monitoring or, even worse, where monitoring is already less than it should be, compounding the problem of inadequate monitoring.

> **There is no such thing as 'computer error' – only people make mistakes**

A less consequential but irritating nuisance is 'automatic billing' for a computer service. This nasty innovation puts the client in the unjust position of being required to review the billing in minute detail because time is charged when the computer decides that a billable connection has been established. Clearly, the computer has been told that if there is a connection, the 'provider' wants money. It has not been programmed to determine the justice of the charge and will bill equally for errors on the part of the server as for genuine use by the client.

'Monitoring'; 'Organisation, Computer'; and the anecdote under *'Contracts, Specifications'*

Contracts

However else the purpose of a contract is perceived, it is above all, a most important form of communication. In this sense, by its nature and its usage, a contract must be absolutely clear. There are two parties to a contract and the agreement must also be fair to both. If it is not, there are sure to be problems and, in the final analysis, the contract may be thrown out by the courts if it is manifestly unjust. Deliberate obfuscation in the terms of a contract may be useful if you are sure that you are shrewder than the other party. However, this is dangerous territory and the project manager should not recommend it to his client.

In practice, there is no true value (but a host of potential problems) in a contract that has vaguely worded terms that may permit a biassed interpretation in favour of one party (even though it be the party you represent). In such a case, the other party (if the sun still rises in the morning and sets at night) will diligently seek and exploit every loophole, indeed, may devote more time to this exploitation than to doing the work.

An example to which most of us who have had renovations done or even a fence installed can relate is that of a construction contract. Unclear and/or unfair terms might persuade the most ethical contractor to assume the minimum quality and quantity; there is no way that the client can avoid this without excessive monitoring cost and losses in time due to requirements for remedial work. Better to be absolutely specific and honest in all the details of contractual requirements and obligations at the outset. Do not, in other words, try to get more from the contractor than s/he is legally and morally obligated to give. You are entitled to expect reciprocation from the contractor.

Many clients and organisational superiors persist in the belief that an unspecific contract will result in a lower estimate and a lower ultimate contract cost. Wrong! Wrong!

This usually means more time spent on writing the contract and sometimes a higher initial cost but it saves time, money and stress in the long term. The higher cost may equally be in terms of time or expertise spent on preparing the contract but also in a higher initial contract value. A contract that contains all the necessary detail (particularly in respect of the scope of work) may be expected to cost more than an incomplete or vaguely-worded one that is full of exploitable loopholes. But the detailed, complete contract pays off in the avoidance of claims for extra work, in avoiding schedule delays, in saving interest charges on delayed payments, in eliminating end-of-contract disputes and in providing the specified product in a timely manner. Each party may even finish the project with a high regard for the other.

The accuracy of the tender price is directly proportional to the completeness of the information provided in the contract documents.

Of course, there are two sides to each contract and you may as easily be on one side as the other. The contractor has to consider that the client is not going to lean over backwards to accommodate the contracted party and there are always financial pressures by the client on the contractor to induce him/her to accept terms that are less than favourable.

The best advice that can be given to the contractor/project manager is to read the contract very, very carefully. Unless it is comprised mostly of a standard form printed and published by a recognised association, read every word and if amendments are made during the negotiation process, read every word again. It is not safe to assume that the only changes made are the ones to which you agreed.

> *A contract format, that had been used many times over, had a blank space for the insertion of the thickness of asphalt in a school playground; it appeared as ½' (a space before the ½') leaving the designer to indicate either 2 inches or 3 inches before the ½. In a particular contract, this was neglected and the contractor claimed for an extra 2 inches of asphalt. Although the error was blindingly obvious and it was argued that the contractor should have sought clarification, he won the argument and with it a substantial extra payment.*

📖 *'Contracts, Scope of Work'*

Diary

Every project manager keeps a diary, right? Not necessarily. Most make a gesture towards it but fail to maintain it as they should. If it is considered as important a task as all the others performed by the project manager, then time should be assigned to its completion on a regular basis. Do not make it the chore that gets done in between other 'more important' tasks. It is necessary that a diary be **complete** all the time. Do not be scriptorially effusive one day and terse the next. Decide on the type and amount of information that will be included on a regular basis and be consistent. Ensure that the diary is completed each day, either as work proceeds and time allows or at a specific scheduled time, probably at the end of the day. If you do it at the end of the day, at least make notes as events occur – a tired mind is not the best tool for recollecting happenings; even recent ones.

A diary note entered several days after the event loses its legal validity as a record and tends also to reflect subsequent circumstances and rationalisations; not helpful in learning the lessons of events. In fact, the sooner the event is recorded after it occurs, the better. There will be no doubt in the mind of the diarist, at a later date, that s/he might have erred and it is then considered a legal record of an event as perceived by the diarist. When being questioned there is nothing more reassuring than being able to say, 'Yes, I made that note immediately, within minutes, after the incident'.

A diary serves as a 'tickler', a reminder of actions to be taken – perhaps its second most useful function. It facilitates the making of a DoList. Take the diary reminders for the next few days or weeks and note them on the DoList sheet as far in advance as serves your purpose, trying to keep the DoList to one page.

📖 *'Communication, Tickler'* ; *'Organisation, DoList'* .

Email

Here is another technological marvel which, properly used, can expedite communications and enhance all phases of the management of a project. On the other hand, there are inherent disadvantages, not because of the nature of the technology but by reason of humankind's use of it.

In the first place, one must accept that there is no such thing as a 'paperless office'. The first danger is that people will rely on email as a method of communication that requires no paper. This is not safe. Hard-copy records are essential. To compound this problem, the ease of use of email tends to increase its use. Newspapers and magazines are full of complaints of the over-use of the medium, of Monday-morning blues increasing exponentially as returning workers face a dozen, scores or hundreds of messages awaiting response.

Because it is so easy to attach a document to a message within the computer, there is a tendency to send, for example, drafts of plans of operation flying through the ether to anyone remotely connected with the project. This may be acceptable as long as the designation of the status of the draft is clear and it will not be mistaken for the next or previous draft. But added to this is the hazard of amendments being made within the document and then flashed back to the originator. It is substantially more difficult to locate and appreciate amendments on a computer screen than on a piece of paper. Gone is the facile opportunity to underline, annotate and expostulate. Yes, it can be done on a computer and there are programs that specify the document status but having been caught in this situation (lengthy attachments), I am not convinced that it makes the job easier or faster in the long run.

Every business **should** and certainly every project manager must establish parameters for the use of email in advancing the project. This is one of the small tedious administrative irritants that, if neglected, can lead to total chaos potentially of such a magnitude that everyone will be shaking his or her head and saying 'But why didn't you … …?' You must work this problem out in the context of the project you are handling but some minimal guidelines are given below.

- Decide what classes of document may be sent by email.
- Establish a clear identification system for originals, up-dates, addenda and all the other variations a document is subject to.

- Make sure there is at least one (permanently filed) paper copy of each accepted or approved level of development of a document.
- Devise a system for indicating within a document what changes have been made (perhaps bold-faced italic with a date and time and originator in brackets, at each amendment).

During planning and implementation, keep a close eye on the use of email and make sure that it is contributing to rather than hindering the project. Take immediate steps to curb its misuse before it gets totally out of hand.

A brief aside on the paperless office. Does anyone still believe that the latest communication and production technology has reduced the amount of paper in use? It is all too easy to photocopy, to fax, to print out email, to satisfy every pathetic request for a copy of ... whatever. Indirectly, the computer is probably responsible for the death of more trees than all the newspapers and books ever published! So go easy on the tree – **print no more than you need.**

📖 *'Communication, Internet'*

Facsimile 1

You may often suspect that fax is still not a completely reliable method of communication. Sometimes there is a feeling that the message has been shot either into outer space or hell.

If you use fax (and who doesn't?), always ask, in the covering sheet, for an immediate confirmation that the message has been received in full, **with a time allowance for the response.** If no response is received, a telephone enquiry is in order. I have experienced a fax record indicating 'transmission completed' when this proved later not to be so. I have also received a fax message directed to a totally different number to a totally unknown person.

It is not enough to be asked (in a fax) that you be informed only if all the fax has not been received – suppose none of it were received. It is easy to mis-dial and send the message astray and, with more and more facsimile machines in use, it becomes easier each day to connect wrongly. The telephoned follow-up is important.

This may seem to be getting a little out of hand. When do you stop confirming that a message has been received and the confirmation has been received? But that first confirmation is essential. All this asking for corroboration may be interpreted as badgering, importuning, bugging (with a substantial risk of unpopularity as a result) and that is what it is. But it works – it gets the job done and it gives the security of knowing that your communication is effective.

📖 *'Communications, Telephone'*

Facsimile 2

A great deal of correspondence is conducted by electronic means. Facsimile transmission (fax) is the closest to the old-fashioned paper communication and some consideration must be given to the authority that is conveyed by a piece of paper shoved into one end of a wire eventually to be spat out at the other end.

No doubt everyone has an example of quasi-legal documentation being sent by fax. In my own experience there are at least:

- letters of intent
- price quotations
- change orders
- offers on real estate
- stock purchase
- minutes of meetings.

How valid are these documents in a contractual and legal sense? To my own satisfaction, I have a legal opinion for my requirements that tells me that contracts may be sent by fax and that the signatures thereon are valid. Such a use of fax should be by prior agreement of the parties. If you find yourself using fax or email in comparable situations, take the trouble to determine the legality of their use for your particular requirements. As with all contracts, there is no problem until there is a problem. Then you had better have done your legal homework – a small expense and inconvenience in the life of a project.

A prominent financial institution with which I did some business is prepared to accept and act immediately on a signature transmitted by fax but requires an original hard copy of the same document with the original signature to follow. They have no hard and fast rule as to how soon this backup must be provided. This suggests that they are uncertain of the legal implications of what they are doing and *feel* better in the familiar context of original paper documentation while prepared to accept that technology has overcome legal niceties – the belt and braces syndrome.

📖 *'Contracts, Legal Aspects 2'* and *'Communications, Internet'*

Facsimile 3

Faxes can now be sent electronically by Internet from a fax-modem. This may not be any more of a guarantee of safe arrival than fax by phone. Holdups by servers can be more frequent than shortage of lines through the normal telephone network. There is also a greater possibility of interception by others on the network perhaps by accident but also by hackers. You will make your own decisions about this method based on cost, convenience and faith but keep in mind that requesting a confirmation of receipt is always a good idea especially if the request is made through a different communication medium..

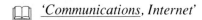 *'Communications, Internet'*

Feedback

This is another management procedure that is more honoured in its omission than its implementation. As often as not, despite that in most organisations procedures exist for evaluation of projects, the useful compilation and review of the information obtained is often neglected.

Projects that are similar in nine and dissimilar in only one of ten hypothetical parameters may provide totally different results. Information and statistics obtained by implementation experience must be evaluated in a proper context of the overall operations of the establishment being served by the project.

Discover, in the planning stage, what provisions exist in the organisation for compilation and analysis of evaluations and incline the evaluation procedures and criteria to serve that norm.

'Monitoring, Evaluation'

Follow-up 1

Always follow up **in writing** on any points that have been mutually agreed between parties or individuals, especially those points that may have a contractual implication – which means just about everything. This will be a natural consequence of communication at a meeting (the 'Action Sheet') but in one-on-one discussions it is equally important. A judgement call is required as to what is sufficiently important to be committed to paper but the project manager is required to recognise this criterion in all his or her activities; it is something that is or must become instinctive in your management skills and practices.

Some contracts, in which changes are recognised as being consistent with the nature of the agreement, require a standard format for changes to be noted and approved. In construction, for instance, a variation order or change order.

Also note the recommendation on follow-up of facsimile communications in the earlier paragraph (Facsimile 1).

📖 *'Communication, Meetings, One-on-One'*

Follow-up 2

More vigorous, more aggressive follow-up is often required in order to ensure that events unfold as they should.

An order has been placed or a report requested and delivery has been promised for, say, a date three weeks ahead. One week beforehand, telephone to remind the supplier or contributor of the date. Three days before delivery is due, call again to ensure that your reminder has not been forgotten and that all the details are correct. On the penultimate day, check again to ensure that the delivery time is established, that the proper address for delivery is known; give any final information. This persistent follow-up applies equally to documents to be provided by a consultant as it does to equipment or materials contracted to be supplied; even more harassment may be required in the former case.

If you are prepared to believe that written follow-up (Follow-up 1) will tend to irritate people, you can well imagine that this will drive them demented. However, it gets results. The number of reminders required and the amount of irritation that needs to be applied depends on circumstances but, in all projects, some degree of stimulation is required to make things happen the way they are supposed to.

> *I tend to carry over this sort of badgering into my private life. I complain at hotels and restaurants if the service is not as it should be – all too frequent, unfortunately. A hotelier, a close friend, confirms that most large hotels have a list of thorny clients and staff ensure that they are provided with such good service as will obviate complaints. It is an unfortunate reality that the squeaky wheel gets the grease in project management, too.*

Follow-up 3

Even more vital, but most often neglected, is the follow-up on activities or events that are not necessarily required to be reported back to management or which may not have an immediately apparent good or bad effect.

A typical case – an instruction is given to a sub-contractor or consultant for remedial work to be performed on a job, a report, a design, a proposal that, supposedly, has been completed. A period during which the remedial work will be performed is established.

Apart from any reminders to the consultant or contractor during that period (depending on the time lapse), management will check with the contractor (or consultant) on the day following planned completion of the correction. On receiving the expected assurance that the work has been done, management then checks with the client, or other recipient, to verify that complete satisfaction has been received. If not, then the whole process must start again but with even more vigour on the part of management.

Assuming that all this process was carried out by telephone (reasonable in the case of small works or minor activities that are performed quickly), now is the time to confirm the requirement in writing with an expression of dissatisfaction at failure properly to execute both the original work and the correction. Other than repetition of the follow-up, the steps beyond this are, of course, the invocation and pursuit of contractual penalty clauses, warranties, bonding agents and so on.

This particular management activity rarely receives its due attention; it is important at all management and control levels. There are usually several hierarchical levels between the sufferer of neglect at the bottom end of the service and the manager at the top. Make sure that the team and staff understand the necessity of following-up and reporting back.

Avoiding the risk of tying project management too closely to construction activities, let me give another example. A consultant (any consultant in any sector) has presented a provisional report that is to be completed to meet a critical milestone. The report contains data provided by a sub-consultant or outside agency; data that justifies the report but appears to contain contradictions within itself. Although the consultant is required to verify the data and tie the confirmed version in to his/her own conclusions, the project manager may not see it until the final report is submitted, probably with insufficient time to check the data again and ensure that a logical result has been obtained from it.

It is incumbent on the project manager or the appropriate member of the team to check periodically that the data is being reviewed, that it does not prejudice the conclusions of the final report and, if it seems necessary, to ask (in a timely manner) for a draft of the corrected data with sufficient anticipation to allow for discussion and resolution of problems that might be occasioned.

The project manager dare not assume that everything will fall into place without his/her constant attention. Nor should s/he assume that the team member in charge will necessarily follow up as s/he should. Frequent reminders are justifiable for everybody in this remedial process in order to ensure that the final report is soundly based and timely. This is not a question of distrust or lack of confidence in staff or team. No-one is immune to error. While the project manager is checking others, there is surely someone checking the project manager.

My first task as Contracts Manager on a large Public Works project was to persuade a contractor to complete some remedial work that should have been done three weeks before. I immediately sent a telegram saying that, if the work were not commenced within 24 hours, another contractor would complete it and the responsible contractor would be back-charged. The contractor complained to the Minister, the Deputy Minister, the Senior Project Manager and, perhaps, the janitor: I was 'recommended' not to send any more telegrams; but the work began next morning as instructed. You will experience moments like this.

Follow-up 4

Equally important as follow-up of **action** is follow-up and communication of **inaction**. It is important that, if there be a hiatus in some anticipated course of events, some unaccomplished activity, a delay, a cancellation, that everyone engaged on or concerned with the project be aware. Make sure that the team, the client and others involved know that nothing is happening, why nothing is happening and when the inaction should end. Just as it is more difficult to find what is missing from a contract than to affirm what is included, so it is more difficult to determine what actions are missing rather than what actions have been performed – either properly or improperly.

> *As a consultant, I asked the project manager if he had followed up on a telephoned request for information. Rather indignantly, he replied that he had telephoned once and it was now the responsibility of the other person to reply. He said he was not required to take any further action!*

It is more difficult to detect unperformed activities than those that are badly performed

---

Graphic communication

It is not yet possible to communicate all thoughts and information graphically but, with computer science advancing ever more rapidly, we may yet achieve that happy state. There is little doubt that symbols, signs, charts and diagrams convey information quickly. Make use of these methods of communication as often as you can in order to enhance presentation and expedite a project. But communicate rationally – do not mystify your audience.

📖 *'Communication, Charts & Diagrams'*

Internet

This is another example of technology potentially overtaking legal context. However, it is more fraught with possibilities of misinterpretation and even fraud than is fax. When does a document transmitted over the net become a final, legal or contractually acceptable document? When it arrives at a terminal? When it has been transferred to paper, perhaps? But has it been modified en route either deliberately or inadvertently? Software can be obtained that leaves hidden markers where unauthorised changes occur but not everyone can afford this nor is it totally reassuring. It is probably small comfort that the United Nations is considering this problem and is expected to make suggestions.

I advise any project manager employing the Internet for any document that has a legal, contractual implication to obtain a written opinion from his or her lawyer – and make sure the legal opinion is on a piece of old-fashioned paper.

📖 *'Communication, Email'*

131

Invoices

When employed as a consultant on the basis of a fee for services and expenses, communication of facts relative to those services assumes an unwonted importance on at least a monthly basis.

Always support your invoice with exhaustive detail. Make sure it is absolutely accurate, of course. Do not claim that 52% of the work is complete if it should be 51%. If the contract is not explicit, devise a method of measurement that satisfies your own criteria and that will survive inspection. There are few things more embarrassing than having an invoice challenged and being unable to justify it.

Omit nothing pertinent from the invoice corroboration. If, for example, you are being paid for long distance calls, list them all with the numbers dialled, times, amounts, any discounts received. This can be done easily by attaching a copy of your telephone invoice with pertinent calls highlighted – and, if you deem it necessary for reasons of privacy, some of the others blacked out.

> **Accurate claims are more readily satisfied**

Typically, this rigorous (you may think, fastidious) detail has two good results and one doubtful. It ensures that you have a system in place that will catch every possible expense and it gives you a reputation for meticulousness in invoicing that, of itself, tends to validate your invoices. At the same time it may, almost certainly will, irritate to a fare-thee-well those required to review and authorise the claim, at least on the first few submissions.

However, as long as you are sure that the information is scrupulously correct and are prepared to say so without hesitation, after the first one or two have been proven accurate, a quick approval is much more likely.

Language

A proper use of language is essential to the successful project manager. If effective communication is the key to successful (project) management, then it is essential to all people active in any sort of business. Unfortunately, it is rarely accorded its proper importance. A surprising number of highly qualified (in some speciality) people are giving instructions, writing contracts and making financial commitments who could usefully spend some time considering comprehensible syntax. This does not mean that we all have to be grammarians or literati but there are standards below which we should not allow ourselves to fall. Given the propensity of the population at large to adopt the latest barbarism of the television sports commentator, we must fight to retain a universal, understandable but correct use of language. I just know I am going to be accused of pedantry or worse! But, because the project manager is, of necessity, an extensive communicator, he or she is in a position to influence a great many people. Please be an influence for good. [Hear, hear! – Ed.]

Role and Responsibility

Consider the misuse of these terminologies. How many times are *roles* and *responsibilities* lumped together as if they were the same thing or as if they were indistinguishable or inseparable from each other?

> **'Role' is the logical result of the definition of 'responsibility'**

'Responsibility' is the condition of being morally (and most likely, legally) accountable for one's actions. **'Role'** is a part or function one is called upon to perform; not the same thing at all as responsibility. It may be said that it is still acceptable to bundle them into the same description; certainly that is much the easier way to handle what may be seen as a problem.

But you will find that the thought dictated by separating them, one from the other, the exercise of determining the true, basic responsibility will go a long way toward assisting in the understanding of the relationships within a hierarchy and between staff and contracted personnel.

Duty and activity

What about *duty* and *activity*? **'Duty'** is sometimes employed as the equivalent of 'responsibility'; it is not. 'Duties', plural, is related to role but is more a description of activities that are obligations inherent in the assigned responsibility. Enough of a difference to be important in both a technical and in a contractual sense.

Shall, will, may

Note also, that the difference in a legal context between 'shall', 'will' and 'may' is sufficient to make it important that they be used correctly.

In January, 1993, the Supreme Court of Canada ruled that a provision of the Income Tax Act was unconstitutional in that it stated that a judge 'shall' issue a warrant. The Criminal Code, on the other hand, uses the word 'may' in respect of search warrants.

The ruling stated 'It is imperative ... that a sufficient degree of flexibility be accorded to the authorising officer in order that justice be done to the respective interests involved.'

This illustrates a rather obvious difference in the usage of 'shall' and 'may' but, perhaps in an obscure context. Nevertheless, it is enough to indicate that misuse of a word may lead to a ruling by a Supreme Court and was perhaps not so obvious as it now seems. 'Shall' and 'will' have different implications. In standard English usage, since the time of Middle English, 'shall' has represented the first person singular and plural and 'will' the other persons, thus:

I shall; you will (or 'thou wilt' – if you want to be a purist); he/she will; we shall; you (plural) will; they will.

This is the simple form of usage as an auxiliary verb and is always followed by an infinitive (with the omission of the word 'to'). My edition of Fowler explains the 'other' usage as being a 'coloured' version with an implication of intent. 'I shall go' simply means that it will happen. 'I will go' implies a determination that the event will occur; (the latter is the 'coloured' application). Anyone really interested in the niceties of this issue might consult *'Modern English Usage'* by H.W.Fowler or *'Usage and Abusage'* by Eric Partridge. Changes or deteriorations (take your pick) in common English usage are not likely to affect the basic legal and contractual implications of these forms.

All of this is not meant to be an abstruse etymological discussion but to indicate the importance of clarity in communication which, by ordering the thought process, will enormously facilitate the writing of job descriptions, the proper preparation of contracts and agreements and the production of organisation charts, leading to effective project implementation. We are talking here of some of the essentials of project management, indeed of all management. Most communications in project management have contractual implications. Be careful how they are stated.

General

This stressing of the importance of using proper language is not a recommendation to verbosity. Using three words when one correct one will serve the purpose is a waste of time, paper and, more recently, disk or hard drive space. It is possible to be simple in the use of language while being explicit. This is not to say that we should limit ourselves to words of one syllable but should choose carefully and be precise in meaning to the extent possible.

As you write or talk, think of what exactly you wish to convey. The project manager carries an enormous responsibility for spending other people's money – it behoves him or her to think carefully before communicating so as not to be misunderstood.

If this all seems a bit over the top, remember that I am talking about legal, contractual implications. You may not know that you have mis-spoken or mis-written until you are slapped with a claim for additional funding or some other constraint that you find equally outrageous.

English is a fortunate language in the sense that it has a multitude of locutions that permit the expression of nuances not innate to some other languages. The danger is, of course, that one has to be more careful in applying the nuances.

Nuances

A careful use of these nuances is important in conveying exact meanings and, as a bonus, makes it possible and useful to say something precisely but with sufficient subtlety that the true meaning is not always immediately perceived. This latter is an artful skill and should be used sparingly, but there are bound to be occasions when a confrontation must be avoided while equally important that a message be conveyed for the record; experience will allow the project manager to recognise these situations. Often this diplomatic approach is acceptable to both parties, saving face while leaving no doubt as to the true intent. Politicians and diplomats do it all the time and who needs to be more of a diplomat than a project manager?

An example of the nuances that may be found either useful or an aggravation depending on whether you need to be subtle or whether someone else is not being sufficiently specific is, for instance, when wishing to indicate varying, increasing, degrees of certainty:

Bob Smith **might** be at the meeting
    Implies – we don't know and it is not that important
Bob Smith **may** be at the meeting
    Implies – we simply are not sure
Bob Smith **should** be at the meeting
    Implies – there are no guarantees but his presence is required and anticipated
Bob Smith **will** be at the meeting
    Implies – there is no reason to suppose that he won't be

Bob Smith **must** be at the meeting
    Implies – his presence is important to success
Bob Smith **shall** be at the meeting
    Implies – THIS IS AN INSTRUCTION

Communicate in both matters large and small as though a lawsuit depends on it

---

Over-meticulous, even pedantic, you might say. But true nonetheless and, if there is a dispute about what was **said** as compared to what was **meant**, it is better to be absolutely sure of what was meant. So make sure that you are clear in all your statements – that there is no probability of misinterpretation. In a contract dispute, such subtleties assume significant importance.

Some people might read these 'meanings' differently but this only serves to illustrate the care that is required in expressing oneself.

Random notes

Except for the first note that follows on 'attitude' (attitude in project management is important), you may be forgiven for skipping these next paragraphs.

- Please give very serious consideration to this one. An attitude that may detrimentally influence the success, particularly the cost element of a project, can be powerfully induced by the casual use of pronouns. It is easy, under the influence of stress and cursory familiarity, to refer to 'my' budget; to say 'I am prepared to approve that if ...'. The use of these pronouns in this sense, with repetition, leads to an easy arrogance of ownership of the resources that distances the origins of the funding further and further into the back of the consciousness. Forgetting or not acknowledging who provides the money all too often can lead to a casual disregard of its value. Encourage all team members and staff to express themselves indirectly, paying attention to the importance of the client as, for example:
  'that may be approved within the terms of my mandate' or, alternatively, *'I believe the client would look favourably on such an expenditure'*.

It matters not so much what is said but the significance lies in the attitude that engenders the statement. This alternative phraseology tends to keep one humble and respectful of the client and the client's money. I have encountered the contrary attitude more often than I care to contemplate, especially in government. The money is not yours – don't become arrogant because you control it.

The balance of these notes include a couple of my least favourite stomach-churners. Although each example may have a management significance, except for the previous one (attitude), which has direct, indisputable project management meaning, you are not required to feel quite so strongly as I do.

- 'Oral' and 'verbal' are not necessarily interchangeable: 'oral', in respect of speech means by voice; 'verbal' means by word rather than image or attitude – it may be written, it may be spoken. Although 'verbal' is often used to mean 'oral', there is a distinction and to avoid ambiguity both words should be used in their stricter interpretations.

- 'Momentarily', according to Fowler, means 'for a moment'. If one were to land momentarily in Heathrow, it might be a rather frightening experience. Landing in a few moments is more reassuring – though perhaps improbable. (I am indebted to Kate Daley of Daley Associates for bringing this horror to my attention.) Likewise, 'presently' to some Scots means 'straight away', whilst to most of the UK it means 'in a while'. To confuse matters more, 'while' to many from northern English counties means 'until' – 'I'll be here while seven o'clock'.

- Do not use 'should' and 'would' indiscriminately. If you mean 'I request it be done', do not say 'I would request it be done'. Avoid raising a doubt in the mind of the listener. There really is a doubt if the listener chooses to perceive it – think about the legal implication.

- 'Hopefully' is still an adverb; it does not mean 'I hope'. One may begin a project hopefully and continue it hopefully but you may not 'hopefully', begin or continue it. Again. this word is much misused but its proper meaning is still current; if doubtful of its use, better not to employ it at all.

- The excessive use of currently fashionable words is painful to the sensitive ear of your delicately-nurtured project manager. For instance, employing the word 'basically' in every second sentence either as a stalling tactic or to give added authenticity to what will follow is usually unnecessary and adds nothing to the thought. It has been so misused in recent years that it has almost lost its proper meaning. Yes, language changes – but must it deteriorate?

- 'Now' still means what it always has – a brief and useful equivalent of 'at this moment in time' or 'at this point in time'.

- 'Imply' means to express indirectly; it is not the same as 'infer' which is what one may deduce for oneself. Unfortunately, there are occasions when, though the error is obvious, it may be defended on the grounds that the speaker might have inferred it – though he did not express (imply) it.

- 'Criteria' is the plural of 'criterion'. There cannot be a singular criteria.

📖 *'Responsibility, Ethics – Accountability'*

Definitions

Some common terms used in project management are defined below. These are definitions based on both dictionary interpretations and experience of a majority of popular usages. Until recent efforts by the Project Management Institute (PMI), project management terminologies had not been sufficiently and so universally codified that everyone could agree with them; however, as long as the usages are common within a project or a programme, occasional variation is not important. The PMI terms will doubtless eventually become the norm.

Action	anything done or performed but in project management terms usually a short-term and decisive action
Activity	in project management terms, usually describes a protracted action or, more commonly, a series of related actions, differentiated from another series of actions within the same project
Beneficiary	the person or persons or group that benefits from the project; may be either the client or those that the client represents
Client	essentially, the person, persons or institution that provides the money or the motivation that makes the project possible or otherwise benefits from the completion of the project; the project manager in a large organisation may see a superior as 'client'
Critical Path	the longest path through a network of tasks that defines the duration of the project; the path that the project manager has to worry about

Duty
what is required to be done, a moral or legal obligation

Function
occupation, office, something performed or done

Functional Management
a system for the control of multiple specialised activities on along-term basis within an established organisation

Matrix
a shape or form across a diversity of different functional units: in other words, a team selected from a variety of functional departments

Milestone
a significant point in the development of a project whereat an intermediate conclusion may be reached and a decision made

PERT
Program Evaluation and Review Technique; a network tool relating tasks to each other on the basis of time and precedence and producing a critical path through the project

Procedures
all the information and activities required to use the system effectively

Program(me)
usually a series of complementary projects all having the same 'goal' within an overall financial and organisational structure ('program' tends to be used only in the context of computer programs)

Project
a project exists as a 'task' entity but not as an administrative entity; this is, of course, in the context of matrix management: it has a beginning and an end (the PMI defines project as 'a temporary process undertaken to create one or a few units of a unique product or service whose attributes are progressively elaborated')

Project Management
the Project Management Institute (PMI) states that project management is the 'management of change' as distinct from 'general', 'operational' or 'technical' management: it is not PERT or CPM or any other mechanism.

Responsibility
the condition of accepting moral and legal accountability for one's actions

Results
are the product of the 'outputs' of a project and the behavioural changes that those new outputs induce in the users of the outputs.

Role	a function or act or series of functions or acts that one is required to perform in order to fulfill 'responsibility'
Task	usually a series of activities that form a completed whole within a greater whole, usually within a project

Mail

I am sure that I am not alone in finding that, with the requirement for expeditious action that is inherent in most projects, national mail services are not always advisable as a rapid, reliable communication vehicle. If you want to be sure that your mail arrives on time, use a courier service (perhaps even a Post Office courier service).

If you must use the regular mail, it is wise to ask your correspondent immediately to acknowledge (by telephone) receipt of any important documents. Follow up quickly on any correspondence that is not answered within a rational period that allows for an assumed, acceptable response time and two-way mailing. Do not simply assume the mail has arrived and that all sorts of activities are being initiated by the recipient.

International courier services are not necessarily as reliable as within your home country. I had courier mail delivered from Canada to me in Portugal. Although the full geographical destination address was given, the courier preferred the post office box part of the address and these urgent documents sat in the post office while the mail was sorted and stuffed into a box for the week-end. Make sure you find out what is likely to happen at the other end. Unfortunately, the courier will probably not be able or willing to tell you.

Mail control

If, within the **project** environment, the responsibility for distributing mail is that of someone other than the project manager, make sure that you change that immediately, either handling it directly, or at least, having it under your control. An enormous amount of time is wasted because the wrong people receive and are expected to reply to communications. (This advice is given in the context of an independently-controlled project: if your matrix is fixed into a larger organisation, you may have to wait, willy-nilly, for the mail distribution system to take its ponderous course before it reaches the project level. After that, all these recommendations apply. But, if you can find some way of overcoming the bureaucratic inertia in the overall system – go for it). When working for the government, I often aggravated the mail-room staff by pre-empting their distribution system by picking up the mail in person.

Make it an early, daily duty to review mail and mark it for distribution. This is another important task, not customarily granted its due value; set aside the required time. Ensure that the principal, accountable respondent is indicated on the item and show a deadline for reply. Also indicate everyone that should be consulted, to whom copies should be sent and give a brief indication of the action required. Something like this:

original:	NB	discuss with JB; reply	(date)
copies:	JB	provide data to KGB;	(date)
		respond and confirm to NB	(date)
	KGB	review, comment to JB	(date)
	DF	review, comment to JB	(date)
	BA	file; tickler for	(date)

Do this quickly; notes written by hand but legibly, please – always legibly. If no-one can read it, it might as well not be written. Copies are made and distributed – all bearing the notes. For electronic mail systems, it might be copied into the computer and distributed accordingly – though it is, unfortunately, easier to ignore invisible mail buried in a computer than it is a piece of paper sitting in an in-tray. Visible paper is more guilt-provoking and, therefore, more effective.

In effect you are creating a small activity schedule within the overall project schedule. Normally, this would do no more than reinforce the existing time-table; but should there be any potential for change in the overall schedule because of your action instructions, make sure that the right person receives a copy with a note that schedule implications be considered and advised.

I repeat that mail distribution is indeed a very important **management** function which is often left to support staff. If the support staff does it faultlessly then they display an understanding of the project process, of the organisation, its elements and their functions: they should be rewarded accordingly – perhaps be considered for a management position.

If the project manager is sure that s/he does not have time for this task, then it should be delegated to the next responsible person on the team. **It must be done quickly, responsibly and accurately**. It absolutely should not be considered a demeaning task, nor be taken lightly nor be rushed through without due consideration of all the implications for the progress of the project.

Experience (mine and probably yours) shows that incoming mail wrongly distributed may sit in an in-tray indefinitely because the recipient can't decide if it belongs there or not; if there is a doubt, it is easier to delay action and, if someone else can be blamed for mis-directing mail, then procrastination can be shrugged off as some-one else's fault. Don't assume that, because this shouldn't happen in an otherwise well-run project, that it will not.

> *After a few weeks as Contracts Manager on a very large project, I realised that mail was being badly and slowly distributed. I instructed staff that I should receive all mail first; then I followed the procedure outlined above. Everyone was so relieved to get proper distribution that my expropriation of authority was ignored (but never pardoned).*

Needless to say, the project manager's copy should go into a tickler file for follow-up and an important follow-up should be noted in the diary. Observe that, in the example, the distribution instructions contain an advice to flag a tickler and that the date should be shown. The mail distributor must indicate the date, being the one with sufficient knowledge of the project to make that decision. Failure to do so will almost certainly mean a delay in response with a consequent delay to the project.

 *'Communication, Tickler'*

Marginal notes

Scribblings in the margins of letters and other printed matter may have an importance greater than their location and legibility proclaim. Some substantial thought may sustain them. On the other hand, they may have been made in an idle moment without thought of their consequence. Avoid this bad habit yourself and persuade your team members to do the same. There are proper ways to handle communication by means of annotations to both letters and other documents. If everyone abides by a certain system, annotations may save substantial project time. The subject is covered more fully under 'Annotations' in this Section.

 *'Communication – Annotations'*

Meetings, formal

When chairing a meeting, politely make it clear at the beginning that speakers must first be recognised by the Chair. Try to stop people rambling (nearly everybody rambles); make sure they address the issues. A knowledge of *Robert's Rules of Order* might help but should not be really necessary, even in an antagonistic atmosphere. Good humour helps in persuading people of the importance of a structured meeting; only be heavy-handed when courtesy, gentle chivvying and wit fail.

Ensure that everyone has a chance to speak and does so. This is especially true at 'approval committee' meetings to which people may be appointed against their will. On such occasions, many people feel an obligation to speak though they, quite legitimately, have nothing to contribute.

Provide the opportunity for each person to, at least, open his/her mouth; say something such as 'I appreciate that this is not your speciality, so-and-so, but can you see any objection from the point of view of an informed observer?' That creates the opportunity to function as a committee member but tends to cut down unnecessary garrulity; it also provides the member with the feeling of a duty having been done.

Time spent in a meeting is no indication of its productivity. Moving to terminate within five minutes of commencement may, on occasion, be more effective in advancing the project than several hours of unfocussed discussion. A lot of dedicated people will thank you for it. But make sure the reasons for termination are valid: there is no room in a project manager's psyche for whimsicality or petulance. The absence of a key member of the committee with information to contribute may be a reason to cancel: there is little point in designing a strategy around information that is not available or reaching a conclusion without having all the facts.

> *Don't treat this matter of members' meanderings lightly. Following a committee meeting at which one very senior member spoke at unnecessary length and to no point, he was asked (very politely) why he did that. 'Well', he said, 'I felt that I had to say something'. Not providing and controlling the opportunity to speak can result in a lot more, invariably pointless, speech than you anticipated.*

Judgement calls will, of course, be required. If someone is absent but other members will not be available for the next meeting, you may have to limp along and come to some provisional conclusions. If this happens, make sure it is properly recorded in the minutes and that the absentee is informed of specific requirements for his or her contribution and the dates the information is required. You may go further and outline the catastrophes that may result from the absence and failure to remedy the situation thereby created.

Quorum

Subject to the cautions mentioned above, if there is not a quorum within a reasonable period of the appointed hour, do not start the meeting. Of course, 'reasonable period' is subjective and depends on circumstances. Normally, five minutes may be allowed at the most. Should you cancel a meeting under these circumstances, almost certainly everyone will be on time for the next meeting. It should not need to be said that the convenor has previously ensured that everyone had adequate notice and a proper agenda and that there are no extenuating circumstances for absence or lateness (a transport strike, a blizzard or an earthquake, for instance).

There is always a considerable amount of pressure from the upper echelons to meet deadlines and they have a similar obligation to be punctual. An incredible amount of time can be wasted while waiting 'just a few more minutes'. If someone is late without some prior notice, there is usually no way of knowing if that person will **ever** arrive; so why sit there waiting? If it is your superior who makes you late for the next deadline, do you think he or she will be sympathetic to the explanation 'Well, it was you that delayed the project by being late'? No, as the project manager concerned primarily with the integrity of the project, you must take the necessary steps no matter whom you offend. You may find that pussyfooting around the issue of punctuality is taken as an indication of either weakness or disinterest.

> *As a Senior Project Officer, I arrived exactly on time for a meeting scheduled and to be attended by my immediate superior and other team members. After 5 minutes, no-one else had arrived. Anxious to get on with other urgent work, I wrote a message on the chalk-board saying 'I was here at 2:00 pm,' signed the message and left. When the meeting was re-scheduled no-one was late – more unpopularity!*

 'Organisation, Punctuality'

Meetings, one-on-one

During and following meetings between yourself and one other (it may be a client or a superior, for example), make diary notes and, where required (for instance, if there is no-one appointed to take minutes), subsequently confirm salient points by written memorandum. If you have done this before, you may not be surprised at how often people resent having their instructions or rationalisations quoted back to them ... *which shows how important it is!*

This, while being an essential management procedure, is perhaps the fastest way to achieving unpopularity ... but also a sure way to being effective.

The written confirmation should be done politely, as for instance: *'in order to ensure that I thoroughly understand your recent instructions, I confirm that I shall ...'* or *'I am sure that a confirmation of the points clarified by our recent discussion will be useful to us both ...'*. (Remember that diary notes made immediately following a meeting, though recorded from memory only, carry a lot of weight in a legal context).

> **At any meeting, silence implies agreement -
> if you disagree ... say so!**

However, employ the technique of written confirmation judiciously: the diary note alone without the memorandum is usually sufficient. On a large project wherein oral instructions may be easily lost to the record, it is important to make sure that they are part of the project history. In a project or organisational environment where self-protection is important you may be forced to resort to the written memo (or at least a memo to file) no matter how much offence it may cause the recipient. *Sadly, self-protection is all too often an urgent priority!*

📖 *'Communication, Follow-up'*

Minutes, 1

The **actual wording** of important agreements or instructions, as they will appear in the minutes, should be decided by those present at the meeting then and there, under the guidance of the Chair (project manager) with the Chair ruling in the event of disagreement. Precision is important; if there is doubt as to the wording at the meeting, the doubt will increase disproportionately on later consideration. If you prefer 'creative' minute writing then you will not relish most of what is written in this book. If you think it is sufficient that a secretary should make the notes without specific instruction, then the same comment applies. The column on the Action Sheet labelled 'Proposition/ Condition' provides an opportunity to present the rationalisations that lead to the 'Resolution'. Because the issues might be controversial, some argument might occur as to its content. If possible the various points of view should also be clarified at the meeting and included in the column *'Proposition/Resolution'*. If the Action Sheet is not to be used, apply the principles that it fosters – clarity, and positive action by a specific person on a specific date.

Critical objections should also be noted and worded with **precision** during the meeting for inclusion in the minutes. This may not be easy, as many objectors tend to object by reason of instinct rather than logic. However, when the objection is **properly and thoroughly** described (as part of the requirement for making a proper record), it can often reveal itself as invalid and may be withdrawn. If it is valid, then it is important, may affect the progress of the project and **must** be properly documented. As a member of a team rather than as a project manager, you may find yourself in the position of having a strong objection to a proposed action; this should help you to appreciate the importance others give to their objections.

Always ensure that required actions are assigned to an **individual** with a date for completion of the action. Allow the responsible person to set/agree to the date or time for completion. This is much more effective than imposing a deadline as most people tend to be optimistic about their capacities. But impose one if you must, as long as it is a carefully-calculated, reasonable, attainable deadline. If the person to whom the deadline applies is not at the meeting, ensure that there is an opportunity for an objection to be lodged immediately after receipt of the minutes and phrase the minutes so this is unequivocally stated, so that it **demands** a response from the person concerned in a specific time-frame.

An action requirement with only a name and no time limit is worse than useless in project management. It suggests that it is important to assign the responsibility to another (passing the buck) but not so important that one need worry that the action actually happen. Be firm – scheduling decisions are the responsibility of the project manager.

Minutes should be formalised and issued within one working day even if it means being hand-written. At least, issue the critical agreements (as an abstract of the minutes or as a memorandum) and follow up with the complete minutes as soon as possible. **Information that may expedite or prevent delay of a project must be communicated to all parties as soon as possible.** Always note on written minutes that objections must be notified, in writing, within a specified time period. (I have been told of an organisation that insisted that the complete minutes be written during the meeting, with a number of carbon copies which were issued as the meeting ended. This might be worth a try – it would certainly make for an interesting meeting – but perhaps a long one).

Remember that, at meetings – silence implies agreement. If you disagree, say so during the meeting; this is another reason for the Chair ensuring that everyone has the opportunity to speak in respect of each item of the minutes.

146

Copy minutes and communications to all those who reasonably may have an interest. It is also easier to copy to peripherally-involved people than to carry the can later when someone says 'nobody told me!' However, the usual warning – do not create useless paper; consider carefully the context of 'have an interest'. The project manager should know what information is important and who needs it. As a precaution, you may poll the team to see if they know of others who might benefit from a copy or who could reasonably be eliminated from the proposed distribution. Do not send copies indiscriminately. If you do this as a habit, eventually no-one will bother to read them and an important message will be missed.

In respect of layout, my preference is to issue minutes in the format of the Action Sheet or sheets – as many as required to cover the subject. It is very much to the point, the inherent space restriction and tabulation outline cut down on rambling prose and everyone can see clearly what originated the discussion, what is required to be done, by whom and when.

📖 *'Communication, Action Sheet'*

Minutes, 2

You may not always be in a position to determine what the minutes contain. For instance, if you are a consultant attending a meeting chaired by another person, it is important to be sure that what you contribute to the meeting and what will be expected of you as a result of the meeting is perfectly clear and indisputable and that the probability of the minutes reflecting that position is the best you can make it. Should the discussions wander down undetermined only vaguely-connected paths without any apparent resolution, it is your prerogative, in fact, your duty to yourself and the project, to clarify the situation and achieve some specific determinants on behalf of all in attendance and those who are to receive the minutes later.

> **Only the uncertain project manager believes that having more information than others involved in the project enhances his or her control.**
> **COMMUNICATE !**

To avoid affront (if that appears the wisest course), say, for example, *'I understand, then, that I am to provide complete data on the soil analysis for the project on (date) and that so-and-so will previously, let us say on (date), have provided me with complete surveys of the areas to be considered.'* Given that everyone accepts this, continue with *'And those are the dates and names that will be entered in the minutes?'* – a rising inflection in the voice as you complete the question and wait for a response.

This can all be said in both a tone and spirit of gentle enquiry; you are the person who just wants to make sure that you fully understand the situation. There is no need to give egregious offence. Realise there may be an inherent insult in the enquiry itself if the Chair wishes to see it that way. The implication could be that the possibility of the minutes containing insufficient information was apparent to you. However, the Chair that does not perceive the need for precision in writing minutes will, as often as not, fail to discern the implication of inadequacy in its neglect. It is difficult to insult a Chairperson who is a blockhead!

Persistence

As a project manager, steel yourself to be persistent; natural modesty or reticence has no place in project management. If you are afraid you may be seen as obnoxious by reason of belabouring a point, learn to live with the misconception. Eventually you will be proven right. The awful alternative is to learn too late, after the project has gone off track, that you should have maintained your position.

A project manager spends a great deal of time receiving and sifting information prior to taking action; it is essential to be aware of the full significance of all the information. It is impossible to enquire too deeply into the information provided. *Listen to this voice of bitter experience; I have been caught out (too often) by accepting that something was so – simply because it was voiced by an expert.* This advice applies in all matters of communication; at meetings, in correspondence, by telephone, fax, email and simple conversation.

An effective project manager **may** be popular but it is not probable – tolerated or accepted, maybe, and perhaps even respected. If you are seeking popularity, better find another profession.

Presentation

It is unfortunate that presentation often, perhaps customarily, assumes an importance as great as or greater than content. Badly presented information, even though of the most exacting accuracy and pertinence can lose much of its effectiveness if the form of its exposition is not both effortlessly explicit and pleasing to the eye.

This applies when making a proposal to a client, when submitting documents for approval to a superior, when making a presentation to the public and any other situation conceivable in which some form of acceptance is required. Your presentation should be accurate, succinct, and eye-catching. Chances of acceptance improve dramatically if you can stun the viewer.

Consider this also from the contrary viewpoint. When the project manager is **receiving** a submission it is important to look beyond the presentation to the content. Modern technology is powerful; computer-generated graphics dazzle the eye and may present great quantities of information not necessarily relevant to a proper appraisal of the data or proposal under submission.

Do not allow yourself to be bamboozled by either science or splendour. Try to see through the superfluous to the essence. Prepare your questions in advance; in many cases, you should already have prepared an outline against which to measure the submission. You know what to anticipate; you know what you need. Make certain you get it.

Neither should you allow yourself to be seduced into acceptance of a document (e.g. a report) because you are acknowledged or thanked for your contribution. Acknowledgements tend to lend authenticity to information and turn aside criticism (it is difficult to complain of content when you are accorded part of the responsibility for it). Generally, those who help or contribute are simply doing their job and no special recognition is required. Should someone volunteer assistance, then a special reference may be merited and included.

Volunteering does not nullify responsibility

My own preference is to eliminate 'acknowledgements' as a traditional, obsolete and self-serving, supposed courtesy. If there is a reference to 'contributors', then those contributors are either in part to be held responsible or should be given the opportunity to declare their disagreement. This applies equally to volunteers as to contracted personnel. Because one gives something, it should not be deemed to be of less value; nor should the volunteer decline full responsibility for the contribution.

> *I am still embarrassed by a proposal I voluntarily prepared for an NGO. I was wary of the concept and tried to steer it into more rational channels against firm resistance. Deciding that I was, after all, just a scribe rather than an originator, I followed the NGO's wishes. The proposal was not a success and my name, though not indicated in the document, was and always will be inevitably attached to it. **I have not done that a second time.***

Records

Make notes of important points of conversations. Keep a **diary**. Make a note of decisions, agreements, instructions, telephone conversations. It may be tedious but, in the worst case, diaries are usually accepted by courts as valid, factual evidence. This is in addition to all those records that you know must be kept – contracts, plans of operation, cost data, purchase orders, delivery notes, telephone conversations, etc. and of which many are usually taken care of by the in-place functional organisation.

> *A manager of times past, for whom we have valid evidence of his care in recording all matters that passed through his hands, was Samuel Pepys. In 1679, Pepys was obliged to resign his post as Secretary of the Admiralty and was sent to the Tower of London on trumped-up charges by his enemies in office. He so overwhelmed the Commission investigating his supposed malfeasances with records, affidavits and testimonials that, although kept imprisoned in one place or another, the prosecution was eventually dropped and he was perforce released. In a time when heads were lopped off quite readily, he showed that a good argument backed by good records can prevail in even the most negative circumstances.*

Nevertheless, the project manager is responsible for ensuring that these records are maintained even though having no direct control of them (assuming matrix management). Someone has to ensure that contract amendments are added to the original document, that plans of operation are modified when policies are changed and that all the possible repercussions of these changes are recorded and everyone is informed. No matter who performs the tasks, the project manager is responsible.

'Communication, Diary' and *'Follow-up'*

Reports

Regrettably, it is impossible to implement a project without periodic reports. Deciding what reports are required, what they should contain, their frequency and who should receive them is one of a project manager's most difficult tasks. If everyone is allowed to decide this to personal satisfaction, there will be a report for all members of the team, their subordinates and perhaps even their close friends! So the project manager must make the decision and risk annoying those people who think they should have a report and annoying equally those who wish they didn't.

Consider the context of the project, its size, complexity, technical imperatives and, as a minimum, decide:

- what information is required to keep each element of the team operating
- the type of information
- the criticality of the element to project success
- the potential for variation in that element
- lag time in producing and distributing reports
- likely response time of the team element concerned
- how the information is to be presented
- who outside the team receives the report
- **how much information is too much.**

Consultants to a government department developed a computerised project control and reporting system at a cost of over a million dollars. The consultants were thorough; interviewed staff from top to bottom of the department. Everyone would benefit from the system. But, when implemented, there was so much information that no-one could separate out their own particular needs. Each monthly report printout stood some 6 inches (15 cm.) high. After a few years, the system was abandoned and another more restricted, better-defined program was developed.... of course, at substantial cost to the taxpayer.

Reporting schedule

A reporting schedule not only serves as a guide for preparing and submitting reports, it also:

- assists in clarifying the plan of operation (POP) for presentation purposes (makes the POP more readily comprehensible)
- assists in developing an organigram
- contributes to the logic of a development and implementation schedule
- contributes to the development of job descriptions
- clarifies contractual relationships.

The chart that follows is an example of a bare-bones reporting schedule for a hypothetical agricultural development project (generally, the schedule will contain many more functional elements and more information requirements).

REPORTING SCHEDULE
ARGENTINA PAMPAS WHEAT PROGRAMME

ORIGINATOR	RECIPIENT	TYPE	CONTENT	FREQUENCY	COPIES TO
Proj. Manager	Client	Narrative Statistics	Progress Data Recommend'n	Quarterly	None
Agric. Advisor	Project Mngr	Statistical	Wheat Production	Annual	Min. Agric.
Equip Supplier	Project Mngr	Statistics Specs Schedule	Equipment consolidation Supply Sched.	Monthly	None
Field Team Leader	Project Mngr	Narrative Statistical	Progress Labour stats Deliveries	Monthly	Delivery data to Equip Super.

Apart from the basic purpose that it serves as a check on reports that will be required, among the many things that the previous Reporting Schedule will clarify are the following:

1. You now know that the organigram must show, at a minimum, the various functional elements indicated in the chart. Project Manager, Client, Agricultural Advisor, Equipment Supplier, and Field Team Leader. There will surely be more.

2. It is obvious that all the activities governing the production of special information on a monthly, quarterly and annual basis must be included

in the plan of operation (POP). This provides a check against the POP as it is developed.

3. When writing job descriptions, there is now an indication of some part of what each functionary is required to supply and to whom. For the Agricultural Advisor, for instance, you will be required to include that s/he shall report statistics on wheat production to the Project Manager annually.

A short report is a good report

📖 *'Responsibility*, Job Description'

Spellcheck

'Spellcheck,' as performed by a computer, does not solve all your editing problems. Failure to re-read every word of what you have written can leave you with some appalling anomalies; anomalies which may have equally appalling legal implications. Spellers, as we all know but may sometimes forget – simply tell you whether or not a word exists in its buried lexicon. It does not say that it fits the occasion for your use of the word.

> *My WordPerfect Speller taught me a new word. I had written 'leat' for 'leaf'. The Speller, correctly, skipped it on two occasions. Fortunately, I noticed it and made the correction. 'L e a t', for those equally ignorant, is a 'crossroad; a water course'. As my father always said, check, double-check and check again!*

Newspapers are particular sinners in this respect, dotting their pages with words that may be in the OED or Webster but have no place in that particular piece of literature. So, re-read the work **after** the spell-check and try to pay attention. After the third, fourth or fifth editing session, I find often that I have read several pages and can't recollect having done so. This may happen to others, even to you. If it does – take a coffee break and go over it all once more. I do not guarantee there are no errors in this book but it will not be for lack of re-reading, spell-checking and re-editing.

📖 *'Communication*, Contracts'

Telephone communications

If you find an interlocutor not available and you want to be absolutely certain of conveying a timely message by telephone, avoid asking that that person return your call: she or he may but, equally likely, may not. To be sure that communication is well and truly established, the only certainty is when you place the call yourself or have it made on your behalf; that is, making the connection must be under your control. This is a nuisance and, it may seem, a time-consumer (it will also be more expensive, especially in the case of overseas calls) but it is much more effective than relying on the interest, the memory or the goodwill of the person you are trying to contact. In the long run, time will be saved and stress minimised because you will know what is happening if you reiterate the call until contact is made.

If the person at the other end of the line says 'I will ask so-and-so to call you back later', but you suspect this will not happen or that it will happen too late for your purposes, dissemble, say that you may not be available and will call again yourself. The offer to 'call back later' by the other party allows someone an opportunity to either postpone an action or to avoid one altogether.

Equally disconcerting is 'I will connect you with his/her 'voice-mail'. This is as uncertain as the old 'call back later'. If you don't really care what happens, leave a message on the voice-mail. If it is important – and it should be, or why bother to call – decline the invitation.

However, when you say **you** will call back – **make sure you do**; even if only to say that you have no information. Keep a diary or written note of the gist of the completed call. Again, confirm any contractually-significant agreements in writing (perhaps by fax – but then, of course, the recipient must re-confirm to you!).

The redial button is a great anti-procrastination disciplinarian: there is little excuse for being put off by a busy signal when all you need do is keep pressing that little button while you get on with your other tasks. Never give in to a busy signal – the other phone has to be hung up sometime and it could be just at the moment that you succumb to tedium. This is one of those seeming trivialities that may be brushed aside as unimportant; but a little well-spent (even if *apparently* lost) time now may save an abundance of time later.

About **call-waiting**. The attitude of the busy project manager to call-waiting may be summed up by a letter to the Editor of the Toronto Globe and Mail. Mr Ted Rowe wrote, 'To be told, 'I'm getting a call, hold on,' is no different than being asked by another party in a face-to-face conversation to stand there and wait while they run to speak with someone else who has just come into the room. Give me a break! The only answer to 'I'm getting a call, hold on, is 'Yes, I'm busy, too. Try calling back when you're ready." Except we know (see above) that doesn't always work either! Is 'call-waiting' discourteous in anything but a universally acknowledged emergency? I think so and so does Mr. Rowe.

📖 *'Communication, Facsimile'*

Tickler

Orderliness demands constant revision of priorities. 'Ticklers' are appropriate in any record system, manual or computerised. They consist of reminders that are progressively up-dated until the action to which they refer is accomplished.

For example, a diary note of a meeting in two weeks time should be recorded on the appropriate date but also, at some time previous, there should be a reminder (depending on its prominence relative to other activities). For instance, on Tuesday, note: 'meeting with X on Thursday'. That is the simplest 'tickler'.

A file, subject to regular use or review, should contain inserts reminding of any activity to be completed. The reminder should be sufficiently in advance to permit the preparatory work prior to the action. This is especially useful as, in the absence of one staff member, another could be lucky enough to stumble on the reminder!

It is as easy to insert ticklers in computer files as it is to establish a daily tickler record but elsewhere (DoList) there is a recommendation that all required actions should be recorded on a constantly updated sheet of paper, eliminating completed actions and moving forward those still to be done. This may be an old-fashioned form of tickler but it is one that is encouraged no matter how good the overall system, and no matter how sophisticated the computer technology.

📖 *'Organisation, DoList'*

A QUESTION OF 'COURTESY'

- When communicating by telephone, do not assume that the person you are calling will recognise your voice or is sitting there with hand hovering over the phone waiting for your pearls. Let your first words introduce you.

- It is both insensitive and unwise to be discourteous to your client (most contracts do not include a 'be polite' clause). A certain amount of antagonism must be expected by the project manager. But if it must be so, make sure that you do not justify it. Do not be deliberately objectionable. If you are, you may be sure that person will get you if at all possible.

- The team must be cohesive. If a member does not like the project, or is on the team against his or her better judgement by fiat of the boss, he or she must suppress any overt indication of this attitude before the client or beneficiary. Make objections known to the team in private not in open forum.

What, you may ask, about my courtesy, the example of my asking 'what would the taxpayers think?' I suggest that may have been marginally discourteous, certainly embarrassing to the committee of thirty but, surely, it was the supreme courtesy to tax-paying citizens.

As an example, perhaps not to be emulated, I like this story of a man who did not suffer fools lightly.

Lord Randolph Churchill, father of Winston, when buttonholed by a bore at a club, rang the bell for a waiter and said: 'Waiter – please listen to the end of Colonel B...'s story.'

5

Contracts

> ## 'Contracts' impact on every aspect of project management

General

During the planning process, the project manager must keep in mind the potential for the development of contractual relationships. These relationships are inherent in all projects; their degree of criticality to the success of the project governs the nature of the documentation that supports and circumscribes the contractual relationship.

A 'contract', in this concept, is not necessarily with an unconnected, disinterested third party – it may include employees within an allied department, within the same company or bureaucracy. It is important that all the relationships for project planning and implementation be conceived in such terms that the agreement to perform the work may be formalised externally by a legal contract or within an organisation by a letter of agreement, minutes of a meeting, acceptance of a procedures manual, etc.

Whether it be a contract to perform a service or provide materials, the relationship should be similar in either case (internal or external) and the terms of reference equally exhaustive. The choice of performer is then open to the most economical or otherwise convenient selection. If, as is often the case, one is obliged to accept into the matrix (see *Matrix Management*) an allied department with an inter-organisational strength equal to or greater than that of the project manager's, when the relationship has already been described in unequivocal contractual terms, the norms of that relationship are already established within the framework of a valid, unarguable philosophy. The pressure to go easy on a related body, to make concessions because of departmental exigencies is eliminated or, at least, reduced. This is important; it is often more difficult to work with familiars than with strangers, especially if they are accustomed to positions of authority, a position of control in their own functional role.

In an existing organisation there are already established hierarchical relationships defined by job descriptions, procedures manuals, etc. Where a team matrix is to be established within this hierarchical system, any variations of function or reporting procedure must be included in the specific job descriptions contained in the project plan of operation (POP). **It is important that these variations be accepted by the superiors that may lose some control of their staff to the demands of the team.** The POP for the project will detail these variations and must make it clear that they are a matter of approved policy within the organisation.

The simple iteration of the proposed status of these personnel in a document that is seen by and discussed by the superiors referred to should be normally sufficient to infer their agreement. Nevertheless, it were better to ensure that the approval or acceptance be confirmed in the minutes of a meeting or by a specific unequivocal memorandum. Although 'silence implies agreement' is true in doctrinal terms, the upper echelons may not see it that way. If there is any dispute about the information having been conveyed, you are likely to be blamed – unless you make sure it is written and communicated.

 'Organisation, Project Team'

Content

A contract must be as long and as detailed as necessary to your specific requirements; **there is nothing that takes care of itself.** The more meagre the content of the contract, the greater the risk to the success of the project. Obviously, the complexity and detail of a contract must be considered in the context of the value of the work to be contracted; there is no point in spending £1,000 to write a contract for a £500 project.

All sorts of documents, rules and regulations may be incorporated as elements of an agreement/contract between parties. Make sure there are references to everything pertinent that may apply. Also take into account the hierarchical importance of documents referred to. For instance, the import regulations of a foreign country could invalidate procurement procedures designed for your own country, a national building code may prevail over a local by-law. Ensure, too, that, when the contract is signed, attached documents are initialled by both parties in order to validate those documents.

It may seem time-saving and useful in a contract to refer to a plan of operation (POP) as a complementary document of the contract; the POP usually contains a schedule which then also becomes a contract document. In any event, all contracts should contain a specific and detailed time element.

However, there are some hazards in referring to the POP; make sure that there is no conflict between the body of the contract/agreement and the POP. POPs are subject to regular review and revision; they are changing documents. References to the POP should take this into account; do not refer to an element of the POP that is a constant variable, without making it clear that the variable exists and the nature of its effect on the contract.

Depending on the nature of the contract, it may be advisable, sometimes indeed essential, to omit the detailed budget from the POP and, if so, then all references to the budget must be either deleted from the POP or a reference made in the contract to the fact that it is not part of the contract documents. There may also be other elements that should not be made available to a contractor or consultant; check this out very carefully.

'Contracts, Duplication'

Contract leverage

Although, in a project management context, a contract is supposed to be an **agreement** between two parties to perform work and to pay for it, in reality it usually represents the terms of an **armed truce** between two entities, each of which hopes to obtain a greater advantage for the effort or money that are the supposed equivalents of the contract.

It follows that advantage falls (at any time during the performance of the work, including the warranty period) to the one who can either hold back on his/her obligation or, by persuasion or shrewdness, induce the 'opponent' to provide more than is legally required. The party's moral advantage increases and negotiating position improves in direct proportion to the amount of financial or work advantage achieved by that party. This is not just a philosophical concept; most contracts work this way.

> **It is a fact that a written contract only becomes useful when a problem arises – so get it right**

So ... **as a client**, make sure that the other party is never overpaid for work performed; in fact try to ensure that s/he is always in arrears.

As a contractor (or contracted consultant), endeavour to gain the greatest financial advantage as early in the project as possible. No need to describe the many ways that this can be done but a large deposit to be paid on the signing of the contract suggests itself as the most obvious, if, perhaps the most likely to be resisted by the client.

This question of leverage illustrates the need for careful cost control and equally careful monitoring or inspection of the work or services – by both parties to the contract.

📖 *'Contracts, Services, Consultants'* and *'Communication, Contracts'*

Contract plan

Perhaps the only certain way to obtain the contract that you want, whether with a contractor, supplier or consultant, is to write it yourself prior to the commencement or even the contemplation of selection or negotiation, in fact, during the planning exercise. This, of course, is not easy. However, if it be done with sufficient anticipation and is modified as the project plan (POP) develops, you will be at least one step ahead of the contracted party. Contract detail can gradually increase. The basic budget will be known; the development of the contract terms will assist in perfecting the budget.

There is no rational reason that, with the proper expertise, a contract complete in all its terms cannot be presented to the selected contractor to be either simply accepted or rejected. Not possible, you may say but there is nothing to prevent working to this ideal; the closer to achieving it, the closer to a beneficial contract. I have done it successfully. Even falling short of the ideal, there is an enormous negotiating advantage if you have considered all the contract possibilities in the detail recommended.

You may be told that writing the contract prior to negotiations will incur additional costs, that you will be giving away the farm. If you don't know what you are doing it may well be true. The assumption is that a knowledgeable project manager with an effective, technically and professionally accomplished team should be able to write a perfect contract.

Your superior or your client may not believe this but you are entitled to expect their confidence. On one occasion that I did this for a government department, a whole hierarchy of superiors had hysterical fits. However, it worked and worked well.

📖 *'Contracts, Expediency (in Negotiations)'*

Duplication

In a large project with multiple documentation, changes made in one section of a record may be missed in another. To avoid this occurrence, which may invalidate a contract or part of a contract, avoid repetition of content where possible. This applies not only within one document (a contract) but between documents that form part of the 'contract documents' or 'contract documentation'.

It is important, when developing any sort of agreement with multiple elements that a philosophy of inclusion be determined as early in the process as possible. Different people or different groups within a project organisation may be working semi-independently to produce a total package. It is easy to proceed 'according to custom' and end up, again according to custom, with a set of documents that either have omitted an important element throughout or that have slightly different variations of the same thing.

Take the time to coordinate elements; take the time to determine what will be included in the sub-divisions of each element and do this to the degree necessary to reduce the work load while, at the same time, inhibiting duplication wherever possible.

An example from architecture:

Drawings must correspond to specifications – but exactly how much information must be included on the drawings? Usually, different people are producing these two elements of the contract. Each must know, **before commencing work**, exactly how descriptive their particular document is required to be. It is not enough to assume the 'usual'.

This is probably as good an example of the danger inherent in duplication as can be found. The draftsman has the same problem within his own drawings. A set of drawings may be torn apart during use but all information cannot be included on all drawings, so it is essential to develop guidelines that will match drawing to drawing and drawings to specifications to ensure that all information is included but that there is a **minimum of duplication** that could create the potential for error when changes are made.

It is better to introduce multiple cross-references into the plan of operation or contract or 'contract documents' than to insert a reiteration or precis of a subject that is covered completely elsewhere. The document will be more tedious to read when completed but it minimises the probability of a change made to one section during document production not being confirmed in another. Take particular care with plans of operation (POP) as they inevitably change. They will affect a variety of other documents, possibly many different contracts. It is in such situations, where there have already been duplications of information, that errors are most likely to occur. Make sure that every element affected by the change in the POP is taken care of, adjusted or eliminated as necessary.

All contract documents should be reviewed (checked) thoroughly, relative to each other, ideally by the same knowledgeable person or persons. This should be done each time the documents are issued and/or amended for re-issue. That means reading **every** word of the documentation again prior to it being agreed and ratified by the signatures of the parties.

This really does mean **every** word; a typo of 'or' written for 'of' can be significant. and has been. *There was a consultant contract of a government department circulating for years, religiously duplicated, with just such a consequential error in the preamble. Fortunately, nobody read the preamble, neither the Department nor the consultants.*

The danger of duplication has not been diminished by the transfer of documents or drawings to computer disks. A central control of inter-related documents by the project manager is imperative. By its nature and by custom (perhaps 'awe' is a better word), a disk acquires an unjustified authority. Because a computer has been directed to put information onto a disk does not mean it is either **correct** or **current**.

 *'Planning, Checking'*

Expediency

The process of negotiating a contract is always difficult and often protracted. There are often compromises to be made by both parties. Nevertheless, there are certain principles (other than legal and contractual) that each party must decide for him/herself cannot be compromised. When the contract is close to agreement and the pressure of time is weighted more against one party than the other, the urge to get on with the job will often overcome common-sense and training, allowing a concession that one knows deep within should not be made.

Such a concession will not **always** result in a catastrophe but it has happened sufficiently often that a good many managers are still squirming in the knowledge that expediency allowed them to be bested in the terms of a contract because they did not abide by a previously-established criterion that they knew for certain was absolutely valid.

There is no sure way to avoid this problem other than to be confident in the knowledge that the terms you have established for yourself are just and necessary; determine the essential points that cannot be modified. Stick to them even at the risk of not proceeding with the contract. Do not succumb to expediency.

Usually, as contract negotiations proceed, each party takes progressive but contractually unsupported steps towards a position that will expedite the project once the contract is signed. The danger here is that one party may progress further towards implementation than the other and so weaken its bargaining position. A confident negotiator will put on a bold front and proceed as though circumstances are, at least, equal for both parties. However, real strength in negotiating is founded on the certain knowledge that you are in the better position.

In support of this stance, ensure that the value of work in progress (feasibility studies, preliminary design, planning, etc.) does not exceed what can be recovered or what you can afford to lose. Budget the front-end expenses carefully before commencing negotiations. Ensure that each disbursement has a corresponding criterion of progress in the negotiations and that this milestone has been fully achieved before the money is released. This is the true test of the character of the manager.

*Our project management consultancy (as a profit-making exercise) developed a small piece of land to accommodate three houses. The houses were designed as timber framed modular sections. The plan was to deliver them to the site from the factory and stack them on prepared foundations. While services and foundations were being installed, the contract for modular units was being finalised. A principal clause was that one set of three modules would be pre-assembled in the factory to ensure a perfect correlation. As contract completion and delivery approached, with money dribbling away, the manufacturer balked at this requirement. Though certain of its importance, the expedient thing to do was to get the units on site. At this stage, both parties to the contract had invested relatively substantial sums. Our project management company blinked first. Of course, the units did not match. Three sets of ground floor units had to be modified on site; winter set in quickly before closing in was completed – imagine the problems. **You may think you are not that much of an idiot – I hope not!***

Consider then that there are three parallel activities or conditions that should be carefully plotted and strictly adhered to in order to achieve a successful contract:

- negotiation progress
- budget expenditure
- confidence factor

The last, which may be the governing factor when all other circumstances are more or less equal, is more than the sum of the first two. Confidence in your negotiating position is enhanced by the knowledge that you are maintaining your negotiation plan; it colours your attitude and becomes apparent to your counterpart (antagonist). This confidence is based on careful planning and a refusal to be stampeded into steps that jeopardise the fixed contractual goal.

Fairness

Contracts must be transparently clear, the terms be obvious. There are two parties to a contract and the agreement must be fair to both. If it is not, there are sure to be problems and, in the final analysis, it may be rejected by the courts if it is manifestly unjust.

The project manager may have to persuade his superiors or client that **fairness is to the ultimate benefit of the project**. There are those who believe that vagueness and skirting around difficult issues in a contract gives an advantage to the client. But, as a policy, deliberate obfuscation in contract terms may be useful only if you are confident that you are smarter than the other party or that you have some leverage such as the threat of withholding future work: however, this is dangerous territory and it is safer to strive to be fair to both parties.

In the case of vaguely worded terms that may permit an interpretation that is biassed in favour of one party, the other party will surely seek and exploit every potential loophole. The project manager and the team will be obliged to do the same – a tedious waste of time and energy for both parties, apart from the potential for additional cost.

 *'Communication, Contracts'*

Legal aspects 1

Always have a lawyer read your contract whether it is a contract you produced or whether prepared by the other party. If there are any changes or additions to the document, follow the advice previously given; re-read every word of the revised document and have your lawyer review it once more if there is the slightest suspicion of a legal nuance to your disadvantage.

You may know how to write a contract; you may be more familiar with the sector and the technical expertise than your lawyer and may contribute to the content but there are some things a lawyer can tell you that can save you all sorts of grief – not to mention a lot of money.

If you take all your contracts to the lawyer (and I mean all), you will be safer and you may be able to establish a fee relationship that will be advantageous to both parties, yourself and your lawyer.

Legal aspects 2

I have been given an opinion that legal documents may be transmitted by fax as long as the originals are kept on file. The opinion suggests that faxed signatures are valid. However, it is wise to include a clause in the first agreement (whether it be a faxed agreement or signed by the parties to the agreement in each others' presence) that faxed documents, duly signed, will be accepted as representing the originals and are valid as contract documents. Of the many situations wherein this may be a great time-saver, it will be especially helpful to realtors who have tight schedules for the sale of properties and for consultants, contractors and their clients for the approval of changes to terms of reference, scopes of work or costs. If you intend to transmit legal documents this way, please first obtain your own lawyer's opinion of its validity.

📖   *'Communication, Facsimile'* and *'Communications, Internet'*

Scope of work

General

A scope of work (the description of the work) may apply equally to contracts for services, for physical works, for supply and/or delivery. The scope of work is, therefore, a requirement of all agreements, to be indicated explicitly in a document (agreement, contract, terms of reference) and, usually, by reference to either a unique formulation (e.g: drawings and specifications) or a universally accepted norm.

A scope of work must, above all, be comprehensive. It must indicate interfaces either **physical or inter-personal**. It must avoid including the scope of something beyond the interface but may refer to it for clarity only; it may have a grandmother/father clause or clauses that ensure that, within the professional or trade norms, there is no room for wriggling out of 'normal' obligations; this catch-all may be included in a professional warranty clause. (see *'Contracts, Warranty'*)

This is an exhortation, indeed a plea, to give as much time as is required to the preparation of the scope of work. It cannot usually be dashed off in a few minutes: it should not be written in isolation from other scopes of work within an overall project plan. If they are all prepared at the same time (in light of the information available at the time) and revised **universally** as more information is developed, the chance of things or activities falling between the cracks is inevitably reduced and, one may even hope, eliminated.

There are cases where this may be impossible or so onerous as to jeopardise the progress of planning. Such a case, typically, would be a design/build contract wherein design continues after the commencement of construction. As many decisions would still be required to be made on materials and techniques, perhaps even on the total area of the building, it would be impossible to write all scopes of work early in the project life. In such cases (as illustrated in the next box), very special care is required to avoid violating interfaces.

An overseas aid project, wherein the contributions of the recipients were either uncertain or known to be variable, could be similarly difficult. But this does not suggest a casual approach to the scope of work but recommends that **more** care be exercised and that revisions be **more** frequent.

> *On a very large government design/build construction contract, as Contracts Manager (under a great deal of pressure to meet deadlines) I inadvertently included some hollow metal, glazed framing in the scopes of work of two contract packages. The same contractor bid consecutively on both and was awarded both contracts consecutively. When we discovered the error during our review of shop drawings and made moves to correct the error, collusion between the Contracts Manager and the Contractor was suspected. Fortunately, the Mounties determined this was not so. The Contractor was eventually convicted of fraud. So, if you want to keep the Gendarmerie, the FBI or the CID out of your hair when writing scopes of work, be careful how you determine interfaces. Fortunately for me, this sort of thing is not a common occurrence – now I am much more careful!*

These notes on scope of work are particularly relevant in regard to contracts involving 'things' rather than services only (though fundamentally true in both cases). Scopes of work for multiple contracts involving supply, manufacture or construction are especially hazardous.

Theoretically, in a construction contract for instance, the scope of work could limit itself to a reference to other documents, drawings, specifications, previous work, etc. It should (theoretically) be enough simply to say:

'Perform the work in accordance with the drawings, specifications and other documents listed in Section X'.

In a few cases, a very few, this could be sufficient (though I have never seen such a one). The assumption is that the drawings and specifications are totally adequate in every particular – an unlikely proposition. The other danger in being too brief is that interfaces may not be adequately covered (see above). This applies not only to construction contracts but to all types of contracts and agreements. As long as there is a starting point and a stopping point, especially where others are involved, there will be interfaces. These must be clearly defined. Two examples for very small building projects follow.

You are proposing to install an exterior door in an existing frame. The scope of work reads:

'Remove the existing door, complete with hardware, patch existing frame as required to permit proper installation of new hardware. Supply door as per attached brochure 'and install; supply and install hardware to manufacturer's instructions. Rub down existing door frame, prime and apply undercoat as required. Paint frame, including interior architrave, to match existing finish. Clean-up and remove debris from site.'

The only additional documentation required with this is a brochure showing the type of door, a similar one for the hardware and whatever contract format you are using. Note that you are not offering to paint the exterior door. Nor are you offering to paint the walls inside the house. Your work stops at the architrave. This is the point of interface with the existing! It is not necessary to say that you will not paint the door – you have not said that you will. The caution is that you must describe the work completely, either by drawings, specifications or scope of work. If there is any part of the description missing that should clearly be there, then the whole scope of work is thrown into doubt and a situation open to dispute is created.

For instance, were 'and install' omitted before hardware, there would be a clear question in the mind of the client. A secure installation would require that the hardware be installed. In such a case (that of hardware installation not being required) the wording that would make everything clear is to state 'supply only hardware'. Simply omitting the word 'install' creates a doubt because common-sense and accepted practice also govern a contract. The General Conditions of the standard construction contract will cover your correcting any damage you might do to other physical elements.

A further example: for the installation of a sun-room where there is an existing concrete slab but where another unrelated contractor is providing carpentry and drywall (gypsum wall-board – GWB):

'The work consists of the supply and installation of a thermally broken, pre-finished, aluminum-framed sun-room with thermopane glazing throughout, all in accordance with the brochure and sketches attached to and forming part of this contract. The aluminum framing shall be screw-fixed to a pre-treated wood sill which shall be attached with appropriate masonry screws or anchors to the existing concrete floor; flashing shall be as shown on the sketch. The sill only shall be caulked both inside and outside with appropriate compounds. Where end mullions and lintel member adjoin the existing building, the aluminum frame shall be fixed, as appropriate, to existing surfaces or to furring provided by others. Aluminum shall be clean when completed to a condition suitable for caulking by others or to receive cover strips supplied and installed by others.'

What I have tried to do in this description is to show that somebody else is involved in the total project and that the limits of this work (project) are clear

– that we don't do vertical caulking – that there is a suitable fixing available – and cover strips are for someone else to install; and that the client or the other contractor have to know that there are elements they have to provide. It also indicates that there is a critical schedule element, in that furring has to be provided before we can complete the work. Don't worry if 'furring' is new to you; it is the principles that have to be established.

A scope of work may take anything from ten minutes to an hour to write for this sort of small project but it can save a lot of argument and, in most cases, a lot of time and money.

> ## Do not neglect a proper work description

Although a construction contract is used as an example, all this applies equally to a consultant contract and especially to contracts with consultants where several are involved on one project. The interfaces of authority and of activity are very important. The coordination element must be clearly shown; in the same way, if there are elements that depend on each other, a reference must be made to indicate precedence of activity. This can be shown in the schedule (if there is one, and there **should** be) and may be referred to in the scope of work – though not necessarily so if it is absolutely clear from other documentation. Nevertheless, an additional reference may not be harmful although repetition has its own dangers.

Many of the techniques described in other sections of this book can assist in the definition of the scope of work and interfaces. For instance, reference to your Responsibility/Activity Matrix Chart can help in preventing overlap of contracts for services while also ensuring that every activity is covered by one contract or another.

Job descriptions in a procedures manual can provide the definition for a consultant engaged on a project by checking the activities of all other positions for interaction (interface) with that particular consultant.

An organigram may be used as a reference to clarify relationships. In the section on charts, you will see that there are clearly indicated interactions between consultants and staff – enlarge on these to develop the scope of work.

'Contracts, Warranty'; *'Contracts, Duplication'*; *'Communication, Charts & Diagrams'*; *'Parameters, Interface'* and the anecdote under *'Contracts, Specifications'*

Related work

Another way of drawing attention to interfaces is to mention 'related work' (or 'associated work', or an equivalent term). While a scope of work for a small project may be simple enough to make clear the requirements of the other players, the more complex the project, the more difficult this becomes; tying related work into the narrative description becomes an exercise in semantics rather than in technical definitions.

You may choose your preferred method of including this feature. A simple listing under the heading 'related work' may be suitable: an advice that *'this consultant must coordinate his work with that of ...'* is another way; or, if you wish to shift responsibility on as broad a front as possible (bad, bad project management), one could say ...

> 'Note that this work interfaces with that of other consultants (contractors, tradesmen); the consultant (contractor, etc.) must ensure that adequate measures are included in his/her plan of work to accommodate these interfaces for the proper coordination of which the consultant (contractor, etc.) is fully responsible.'

This latter, of course, is an abdication of responsibility and puts you in the position of having to apply the warning across a number of related contracts, making each of the contractors or consultants responsible for coordination. It temporarily gets you off the hook to a certain extent but by splitting the responsibility for coordination or multiplying the responsibility, it tends to create more obfuscation than light. It is a methodology that cannot be recommended but is all too often used, although perhaps not to the degree indicated in the example. In the long run, avoidance of project management responsibility can only result in arguments, possible lawsuits and unnecessary expenditure.

It also ignores the fact that the consultant or contractor may have no better 'plan of work' than to do it the way it is always done. While this may be sufficient to obtain a completed project, it does not lend itself to expeditious implementation. The project manager has a responsibility to do more than protect his position and shift responsibility to others. The project comes first and, if this or similar avoidances of that responsibility potentially may cause delay of even one day or in any manner whatsoever jeopardises the project, then the project manager must take more positive steps; must, in fact **describe the work adequately and avoid cop-outs.**

Exclusions

There is a real danger in listing 'exclusions' (work to be done by others) though it is often done. How should you approach 'exclusions'? Do you take the 'likely' things that may be mistakenly included in the work? Or do you stretch to the 'probable', 'improbable' or 'highly improbable'? Who defines these terms? Is it possible that any two people would agree on 'likely', even though most people may agree on 'obvious'?

A well-written scope of work includes **everything** required. If you are not sure of what should be in there, where do you draw the line as to what should be excluded? Try to avoid this pitfall; spend the time and effort and obtain the technical expertise required to prepare a **complete** scope of work. In my own experience, they are too often written at the last minute in too much of a hurry.

Services, consultant

A contract for consultant services needs to be as comprehensive as one for works or supplies. There are a good many extant examples of the basic elements of this type of contract and they present no major problems. The same cautions apply in respect of the scope of work. (See '*Contracts, Scope of Work*' & *Appendix, Consultant Contract*).

However, what is often found to be missing in most consultant contracts, or at best inadequate, is a **sufficient** indication of the method of measurement of the services, criteria for determining when payments should be made and how much each payment should be.

For instance, a contract for 'architectural design services' is often defined in terms of percentages of completion of the work. While there are certain generally understood broad criteria for measurement in this type of contract (concept, sketch design, preliminary design, final design, working drawings, and so on), there is, inevitably, a substantial degree of subjectivity in the appreciation of these degrees of accomplishment. The difficulty is increased in most such cases because there may be a need to judge percentages of completion of several subdivisions of the work – which means percentages of percentages!

A Le Corbusier sketch (or a Frank Lloyd Wright sketch if you prefer) handed to an executive architect might have comprised only 1% of the paper to be produced but constitute 80% of the conceptual thinking. In such a hypothetical case, what would be the fee, were the project to be terminated at that stage?

Fortunately, most of us will never have to make such a frightening decision (in any event, Le Corbusier would have made it for us). What is important in our more ordinary world is to take whatever steps are possible to eliminate the **need for subjective decisions** when measuring work completed; which means **defining these criteria in as much detail as possible**, in the contract. This is definitely not a simple task.

It cannot be assumed that the project manager will always have the technical capacity to judge completion stages nor to be able to originate the standards. This usually falls to the team member with the appropriate professional background but the project manager can, must make sure that there is an awareness of the need for a rigorous consideration of these factors.

In addition to the technical parameters for determining basis and method of payment in contracts for services, there are certain key contractual criteria to be considered, for which guidelines follow.

- Do not assume that there is a minimum percentage that must be paid at any one stage; if you judge as little as 1% appropriate, then make it 1%.

- There is no maximum number of payments; within the context of maintaining a reasonable monitoring and administration cost, split the payment schedule into as many parts as appear to fit the stages of the work production schedule.

- There must be a thoroughly comprehensive description of each stage so that there is no ground for dispute when payment is made.

- In judging the stage completion, quality is as important as quantity; completion means just that. It must meet the standard of work specified – in every detail.

- Where possible, include a contract clause that permits cancellation at completion of each stage of the contract.

- Include an unequivocal schedule of production: one of the possible consequences of not meeting the schedule should be cancellation of the contract, at the discretion of the client.

- As often as possible, include the phrase 'to the complete satisfaction of the client'.

- Include 'client review/approval' stages that, advantageously to the client, may be more frequent than payment stages – although your review costs are still a factor.

- Do not tolerate claims for additional cost beyond what is contained in the contract or contract stages: this, of course, presupposes that the contract stage descriptions are complete and comprehensible.

- Ensure that there are detailed payment rate schedules in the contract for possible additional work initiated by the client or that such a possibility is totally excluded.

- Ensure that any and all documents attached to the contract are initialled by both parties and dated.

Although this illustration is in a different category to contracts for consultant services, nonetheless, it applies as an example of what may be made acceptable as an alternative to following the 'customary' practice. Residential construction contracts in the Algarve (Portugal) were usually paid in 3 or 4 stages. In contracts that I wrote, I introduced 17 stages (each rigorously described), thus tightening cost control and scheduling. Contractors were quite happy with this arrangement as it improved their cashflow, although the true objective was to avoid overpayment by the client. Of course, inspections (monitoring) increased but the potential for loss due to error was significantly reduced for both client and contractor. Remember – be fair to both parties.

The view from the consultant's perspective is modestly different to that of the client. There should be no objection to any of the stipulations above but a contract has to be fair to both parties not only in the terms in which it is written but in the respect for each other that is manifest in its practical application.

The inclusion of 'to the complete satisfaction of the Client' is a fair condition as long as it is clearly established what it is that has to meet this criterion. A consultant is often in the condition of being hesitant to refuse a contract no matter that the terms are not entirely satisfactory. There is a risk in refusing but often a greater risk in accepting. A consultant contract that keeps the consultant working for months or years at an increasing financial loss is not a tempting contract.

**Vague terms of payment are not beneficial
for a contracted consultant**

I caution any consultant against giving what amounts to a 'free sample'. Try to avoid commencing work before the contract (or, at least, a letter of intent) has been signed. It may ingratiate you with the client to begin the work without essential security but it carries the danger that you may never get paid. It also encourages the client to be dilatory and strengthens his/her control of the contract.

Appreciate the value of your own work; develop your own 'fair' contract against which to measure that proposed by the client. Before commencing negotiations either of terms of reference, performance criteria or fee schedule, prepare draft versions for yourself, especially of the fee structure. If your work is consistently the same product, all this should be easy enough and at your finger-tips. If there is usually a substantial variance between each of your contract Terms of Reference (TOR), make an extra effort to prepare for the negotiation process.

Time is well-spent before and during contract negotiation and may save days or weeks of wasted labour during implementation or when the contract is, in your opinion, completed – and when the nasty contract component of collecting the money begins.

**It is better to lose a contract than to lose money
on a contract**

Perhaps, for the consultant, the most important point to remember is to break the progress payments down into sufficient production packages to ensure that cash flows while the work is being produced. Do not continue the work until your production to the date of invoicing has been acknowledged in writing *(preferably in writing on a cheque!)*. It is not easy to be unforthcoming with a client but remember that you are also a businessman or businesswoman; you will not remain a businessman or a consultant if you work without pay.

It may be argued that it is not simple to break down, let us say, a feasibility study into recognisable and remunerable elements. Agreed, but I make the point that it is worth using all your ingenuity to do so if you wish to maintain a viable consultancy. Time spent on such an analysis will be well rewarded if it provide you with a reasonable, sustainable cashflow.

Assuming that you know your subject thoroughly, this should not be an unsurmountable obstacle. It is also a distinct advantage to the client – though rarely appreciated – in that it provides approval milestones and clear indications of progress.

Although I mention hourly rates for additional work, I have assumed that a consultant contract will usually be founded on a lump sum or known cost basis. My opinion is that this is most satisfactory to both consultant and client. The client knows what the ultimate cost will be and can budget accordingly. Similarly, the consultant does not have to justify every minute that s/he or staff are working. Open-ended contracts are generally unsatisfactory.

However, they are sometimes unavoidable. In such a case, great precision is required in monitoring the work. Everything above applies but 'in spades'.

📖 below: *'Specifications'*

Specifications

Specifications, scopes of work and terms of reference all have something in common and might even be either confused with each other or actually replace each other. Briefly, 'specification' is a detailed statement of the particulars or nature of the thing or service, a **description** of what is required or, for that matter, what already exists.

A 'scope of work' describes the magnitude of and what is to be included of the thing or service. It should not describe the nature of it (that is the specification).

'Terms of reference' (described later) reflect more closely the scope of work than the specifications. In the box on the next page, you will see an example of the use of 'specification' and 'scope of work' to mean the same thing. But what is much more important in the example is an indication of what can go wrong (appallingly, incredibly wrong) if either the specifications or the scope or the terms of reference or the description or the plans, or whatever they may be called, are inadequate.

Whichever of these descriptive elements you are using – and it may be more than one – they must be given due thought or there will be arguments, delays, financial losses and, maybe, court cases.

See the box on the next page ...... and ...

📖 *'Contracts, Terms of Reference'*

One of the largest software design companies in North America (USA and Canada) had problems with a contract performed for the Government of Canada. Eventually the contract was cancelled. The Senior Vice President of Delivery Services (of the design company) had this to say, 'In this case, it took a long time to realise we had such a wide misunderstanding between the two of us on the nature of the scope of the work they really wanted to have done'. He went on to say, 'If there was a lesson, it might be: Try to be clear on the specifications when you start. And if you realise that you do have a difference of opinion, then deal with it really quickly, rather than letting it drag on'.

*What is **frightening** about this is that it happened in the mid-nineties. Contracts have been around for thousands of years but we are still struggling with inadequate descriptions of the work and/or scope and with an inability to make those small decisions that can save or ruin the project. Even more frightening is that some of the worst offenders (who clearly identify themselves) are governments and technology whizzes.*

*Incredible but true and reported in the Toronto Globe and Mail. This was a multi-million dollar contract between a government stuffed with bureaucrats and a modern, prominent software designer with a reputation as an industry leader. Neither party was aware of the inadequacy of the scope of work: neither party knew that a difference of opinion should be dealt with quickly! It is hard to believe that two such basic criteria for effective management had not simmered to the surface in years of operation for the company and centuries for the bureaucracy. Here you see a contract failure because of elementary ineptitude (when, in fact, it should all have been 'incredibly easy'). **Clever people all too often lack that basic essential of good project management (and just plain management) – common sense.***

Terms of reference (TOR)

This expression is generally applied to a contract for services corresponding in some of its elements to a scope of work. Essentially, it is a description of the relationship between a client and someone providing a service, though it may be within an organisation (terms for a special mission or task) and, therefore, not requiring a fee structure – but certainly a budget.

In the latter case, the TOR should be as complete as possible, within the framework of an already existing employer/employee relationship. That is, whatever is special about this task should be clearly set out, including accountability, special objectives, activities to be undertaken, reporting procedures, etc. It is a contract within an existing employment contract.

📖   '*Contracts, Specifications*'

Warranty

Warranty clauses are standard in most contracts: they are more difficult to formulate, more difficult to assess and more difficult to enforce in contracts for services. Nevertheless, they are important if for nothing more than an indication that the client has given the subject consideration and is prepared to demand compliance with the terms of the contract. The standard of compliance could be, for instance, a professional code of ethics or generally accepted standards of workmanship within an industry. This norm is additional to an explicit description of the work itself and inherently implies the exercise of 'reasonable skill and care'.

Example:

The Consultant warrants that she is competent to perform the services required under this contract in that she has the necessary knowledge, skill, training, available time, technical, logistical and other resources to perform the services. The Consultant agrees also that she shall perform the work to a standard no less than that required by the professional association, or other authority establishing standards, of which she is a member in good standing or to which standards she subscribes and that the work shall be completed in accordance with the terms of the contract and to the complete satisfaction of the Client.

I introduced this clause into consultant contracts I originated when I worked for a government department. I am happy to say it was adopted and appeared in my last consultant contract for them.

There is no harm for the client in the repetition to the point of boredom, throughout a contract, of the phrase, vague though it may seem, 'to the complete satisfaction of the Client'.

Should a problem arise, it might be necessary to refer to the professional body invoked. However, such difficulties are rare because reputable professionals are aware of their responsibilities. Nevertheless, reinforcement by the inclusion of the warranty clause is salutary. Do not neglect it.

One basic assumption in respect of compliance with the terms of a contract and the determination of the need to invoke the warranty clause, is the importance of being able to recognise compliance or its absence. It is essential that members of the team monitoring technical or professional performance be in a position to make a judgement. It is no good being dissatisfied in a vague way with a consultant's work unless you are able to justify the criticism with facts, figures and alternatives. This does not mean that all the team members have to be technically smarter than their consultant counterparts (though that helps) but that they should have a sufficiently broad experience of results and the method of reaching them to make a judgement call possible. If not, employ another consultant to watch the first consultant. More costs it is true; but the savings can easily outweigh additional expense. (See the box under '*Specifications*', above.)

DUE FOR ANOTHER BREAK !

6

Monitoring

General

The importance of monitoring to successful project implementation and completion cannot be over-emphasised. Its benefits are usually not appreciated at any management level and, often for reasons of cost, it is reduced in scope or, regrettably, neglected altogether. Full consideration must be given to the need for constant, diligent, competent monitoring during all project planning because:

- inadequate or ineffective monitoring is a major factor in the failure of projects, second only to inadequate planning

- properly performed, monitoring provides, in one basic function, current supervision and **timely opportunities for remedial action** (it is always advantageous if the 'monitor' is authorised to prescribe remedial action on the spot)

- proper monitoring of costs will invariably save more than the cost of the monitoring itself

- final project evaluation is substantially simplified by the accumulation of information acquired during monitoring activities. In fact, each monitoring inspection may be considered a milestone or phase evaluation.

The indispensability of adequate monitoring is a difficult concept to sell to management. It is usually more of an afterthought than a planned activity; or it may be thought to be a natural and always-present concomitant of management, so not requiring special consideration or funding. Even though it may get the nod from client and superior in principle, when defined in detail, its inconvenience and cost tend to overshadow its utility. Do not be dismayed when encountering opposition; this is where your 'attitude' as a project manager will be put to the test; you must believe in your heart in the importance of monitoring. If the project is to succeed, it is worth putting out extra effort to ensure adequate, appropriate monitoring.

> *As a monitoring consultant, with authority only to advise and recommend, on projects sometimes 12,000 kilometres (7,000 miles) from head office, I generally managed to achieve contract compliance, by saying 'I have no authority to instruct you but my report will contain a strong recommendation to do such and such. You could save a lot of aggravation and money by doing it now.' If it seems obvious that you know your subject, there will rarely be a problem.*

Budget for monitoring

No two projects require the same intensity or amount of monitoring and a precise magnitude of costing accuracy can only be achieved as the project plan is developed and its range of activities and its complexities become clear. For which reason, because monitoring costs may vary substantially from project to project and **because they are a direct consequence of the project development**, such costs should always be included in the project budget. They should not be seen as an administrative cost additional to or separate from the project.

Also it is more cost-effective and makes for simpler strategic/programme budgeting if monitoring costs can be increased or decreased within a cost-limited project package by balancing other project expenditures to avoid cost overruns. Be aware that monitoring usually costs more, often much more, than many clients (and most project managers) anticipate, which is not to say the costs are not justified but rather are ignored or evaded in order to maintain maximum available funding for what are considered the 'real' benefits of the project. But these 'real' benefits are not likely to be fully realised in the absence of proper monitoring.

In the same way as for contingencies, unused monitoring funds may (**should**) legitimately be transferred forward for later disbursement for the project or added to the contingency fund. Strive for this flexibility when preparing the plan of operation. As long as monitoring costs are considered as part of the project budget, this should not create a problem of perception for the client or the boss.

In order honestly to justify monitoring and to take advantage of its flexibility the project manager must be very careful how these costs are calculated. Make sure that your cost proposal will stand up to the most exigent questioning. Having acknowledged that monitoring is difficult to defend, being unprepared when required to do just that will call into question the validity of your total plan of operation. But remember what I said earlier in this section. ... *The indispensability of adequate monitoring is a difficult concept to sell. It is usually more of an afterthought than a planned activity ...*

Ontario Hydro is one of the largest public utility companies in North America. Over the past few years it has been found dangerously delinquent in many practical and managerial respects. The Government of Ontario has committed itself to straightening out the mess.

A report in the June 1999 issue of Globe and Mail Report on Business considers the question of untendered Ontario Hydro consultant contracts. Some frightening examples are given. One consultant in particular was paid $136,000 and produced a two and a half page fax. The Hydro President, when asked about the contracts in an interview said, and here I quote the Globe and Mail article, 'that untendered arrangements are common in the business world.' He added that he was 'baffled by this notion that every piece of work that's done by a consultant should somehow be written.'

Now, he is quite right that every piece of work does not need to be tendered. It depends on the value of the contract and the perception of conflict of interest. Nor need the results always be submitted in writing. But there should be, at least, (monthly) reports, time sheets, expense details, some sort of paper trail. This is the public's money. It is always someone else's money. If the consultant refuses to write reports, then it is the responsibility of the person to whom he or she is reporting to make sure that there is a record of the advice given or the activities undertaken. *(cont)*

> *In any event the contract, untendered or not should contain a reporting requirement. Remember that managers and project managers are working for shareholders, taxpayers or donors.*
> *Why should this interest you? It shows that management in even the highest places should not be complacent just because things seem to be going well and no-one is complaining. Monitoring should be a constant process. Ask questions, look into even those operations that are apparently running smoothly. Do not wait for a crisis. There can be a great many unpleasant things hidden under nice-looking rocks.*

📖 *'Parameters, Contingencies'* and *'Monitoring, Schedule'* and *'Budget'*

Checking

Checking and cross-checking are important throughout the life of a project from planning to completion. Although the project manager is ultimately responsible for the integrity of his/her work and for the project itself, it is important that s/he ensure the accuracy of every contributor and every contribution to the project; this includes the project manager her/himself and the work s/he produces. Do not be ashamed to have your work corroborated or corrected by others.

This is, in effect, self-monitoring and, while the responsibility for the accuracy and integrity of the project plan and the project implementation cannot be evaded by the project manager, some reassurance can be gained from another person's viewpoint.

📖 *'Planning, Checking'*

Criteria for monitoring

Factors to consider in determining the magnitude and scope of the physical monitoring element of a project are:

- cost of access to the project
- complexity of the project
- variables in required monitoring expertise
- skills and breadth of experience of project implementation personnel
- management's familiarity with and confidence in the implementing team

- monitoring cost relative to the cost of the project
- potential for injury to the project due to delays in both reporting and responding.

Evaluation

Many of the subjects discussed in this book could themselves have a complete book written about them; evaluation (the assessment of the validity of the project plan and the consequent success of the project itself) is one. While it is a complex subject, there are certain basic points that the project manager should keep in mind when considering evaluation:

- establish success parameters during the planning stage
- make sure the parameters are measurable
- monitoring should be considered part of the evaluation exercise, so establish interim evaluation criteria to coincide with monitoring milestones
- use the Logical Framework Analysis as a guide to evaluation requirements
- a most important element of evaluation reports is the recommendation for improvements; the next project should benefit from the failures of the last.

All too often, valuable information is filed and forgotten. Make sure that evaluation criteria and methodology conform to any existing information consolidation procedures of the organisation for whom the project is being developed. Or try to ensure that **your** criteria and methodology will be accepted as the revised norm where they do not already exist or as improvements where they do exist.

Some people see success parameters as 'failure' parameters. This is true to the extent that not meeting with success implies failure. Nevertheless, the parameter will not vary, no matter its name, and the more positive terminology contributes to the spirit that inspires the project team.

 *'Communication, Feedback'*

Inspection (especially construction projects)

Inspection, as it applies to construction work specifically, is usually underrated, under-budgeted and misunderstood by management. It is often, wrongly, seen as the operation that slows down the real work. By extension, this applies to any project that calls for inspection, be it a contract to supply goods, establishment of a health service programme, the development of a control system or anything that fits the definition of a project.

The unthinking disregard for inspection/monitoring and the reinforcement of its neglect is perpetuated often by unhappy experience originating in inspection that was inadequate in scope and, when performed, most often in arrears of time. The consequence of that neglect is usually a requirement for remedial work, resulting in a bad name for inspection (monitoring) rather than, as it should be, for poor workmanship and poor management.

Properly implemented, inspection has to permit the inspecting staff to monitor the work as it is performed and the extent of the inspector's work must not be so great as to prevent complete, timely coverage of all his assigned tasks. Simply put, make sure you have enough inspectors!

The inevitable result of giving proper importance to inspection is, of course, an inescapable **increase in inspection costs**. However, it beneficially minimises remedial work, accelerates progress and **reduces overall costs** of the project.

An early understanding of this by both client and contractor before the commencement of the project will benefit both parties. This is particularly true in the present construction environment of multiple sub-contractors with a general contractor performing coordination, some supervisory activities and little else.

There is a routine misunderstanding (originating in hope and faith rather than experience) that, because there is a contract or contracts, then compliance with the terms of the contract is automatic, that the general contractor or other supervisor need do no more than **anticipate** compliance. Unfortunately, this is far from true: if there is no inspection, you can be sure that compliance will be at best spasmodic and certainly variable. You cannot afford to rely on the goodwill of the other party to a contract, to any contract. You must ensure compliance by regular, thorough inspection. This is realism – not cynicism.

Inevitably, the question of 'aptitude' must be raised. An inspector who waits for a job to be performed wrongly before ordering it either stopped or corrected is neither going to expedite operations nor save money for either party to the contract. Being 'right' is not enough – we are all trying to complete the work both correctly and expeditiously.

> *An example of successful monitoring (inspection) that some might think excessive was in the construction of an airfield in wartime conditions (WW II). In each section under construction, each trade foreman and his team was monitored, on a full-time basis, by an expert in that trade. At any sign of bad workmanship or doubt about method, the work was stopped, advice and a decision sought. This created many more stoppages than usual but of minimum duration, while eliminating the usual need for remedial measures after completion. The airfield was completed ahead of schedule. Yes, there was project management in 1943/4!*

The first requirement of an inspector (monitor) is the knowledge of techniques; the second is the ability to discuss operations with contractors, artisans and operatives, indicate diplomatically, through proper channels, what will be tolerated and what will not, and impose standards without creating animosity. Staff of this quality are not easy to find and not cheap when they are but they are worth their weight in completion schedules.

All that has been said above applies, in principle, to all projects, not just construction projects; the variable is the monitoring schedule. Some projects will require constant supervision, some will require inspections on a monthly basis, others at irregular intervals. The project manager must not neglect to give this full consideration. The proper technical skills and personality requirements of the inspector/monitor are also an essential prerequisite.

Monitoring and strategic planning

Certain types of established organisations (e.g. NGOs – Non-Governmental Organisations) with a project orientation that acknowledges the importance of monitoring, can make a case for a policy of seeking or developing projects in a smaller geographical area and directing efforts to a special sector of development or enterprise in order to concentrate the monitoring expertise required into the minimum number of persons.

Consideration of monitoring then becomes an essential factor, perhaps a limiting one in respect of scope of operations but also a potentially cost-effective factor in the success of projects and, consequently, of strategic planning decisions. It may happen that economics alone may preclude adequate monitoring in the field on a sole-project basis but monitoring trips can often be justified by coordinating those activities to include a number of projects.

Monitoring is required of both field/site and headquarters operations. The nature of the project determines the emphasis. Example: working in an overseas environment, a project that encompasses the consolidation of materials from a multitude of head office (home country) suppliers may require an emphasis on monitoring at home with a minimum of input at the unloading point. Conversely, a known procurement firm in the home country may be so efficient and inspire such confidence as to minimise the need for monitoring except at the overseas delivery point.

> **Monitoring, properly planned and implemented can substantially affect strategic planning criteria. At the same time, it can materially improve cost-effectiveness.**

These are important value judgements and may have a significant effect on the success of the project and its overall costs. In a matrix environment, headquarters management should also ensure an internal project monitoring system beyond the normal functional management control. A 'Project Review Committee' (which, depending on resources, may comprise only one person – one not involved in the project) should monitor progress on a regular basis and be responsible for assuring that field operations are proceeding properly, that there is proper coordination between head office and field and that proper project-specific financial and activity records are being maintained. It is better that such a committee not have authority to instruct but only the right to recommend. But take into account the time and cost implications of such a committee – such monitoring, properly performed, is no small task.

📖 *'Monitoring, Inspection'*

Schedule

Do not obscure or dismiss the need for project monitoring in order to gain approval of a project; if you believe in its importance (as you certainly should), make everyone aware immediately of the requirement and develop an accurate indication of its magnitude as early as possible. If you decide to put in a high estimate as a 'cushion' you may find the monitoring element rejected out of hand; should you try to make its cost acceptable by deliberately underestimating, it may be impossible to increase its budget later in the project, thus jeopardising successful completion. So spend the time required to consider all applicable factors and make as accurate a calculation as possible. This is not easy in the early planning stages but it is an essential skill that the project manager must develop.

Project proposals, as well as plans of operation, should always contain a monitoring/evaluation schedule (cost may be calculated separately) indicating:

- frequency
- personnel required
- special experts or expertise required
- cost per inspection (including travel costs and other expenses)
- elements to be reviewed/evaluated
- results anticipated.

To simplify the schedule, descriptions of the staged success parameters may be indicated in the plan of operation rather than on the chart.

Detail and complexity of the information presented will increase during project planning. At the proposal or feasibility stage, a simple chart is adequate. For a plan of operation, cost calculations and monitoring rationale should be detailed (in a separate tabulation, if necessary) as support material for the activity chart.

The chart is a simple but essential aid to understanding of the basic project elements. Part of a limited schedule is shown in the following example.

MONITORING SCHEDULE

Officer	Month 1 Site	Month 3 Factory	Month 4 Site	Month 9 Shipper	Month 12 Site	Month 16 Site
Project manager	●					●
Agronomist	●		●		●	●
Procurement officer	●	●		●		
Procurement monitor	●	●		●		●

In this hypothetical and deliberately incomplete example, there is no special rationale for the choice of monitoring period nor for the length of the project; these variables depend on the nature of the project. The project implementation schedule governs which officers or consultants should visit site, factory or shipping assembly point and when.

Keep team or group visits to a minimum. I have found that more is accomplished when one **reliable, experienced** officer or contracted person, properly briefed, performs an inspection alone, unless the expertise of several team members is absolutely essential.

If the project manager is not present but more than one inspector is involved, **make sure that there is a nominated leader** and that his/her authority is clearly established. This means that special terms of reference (TOR) should be prepared for the monitoring visit, especially if decisions are to be made at the site; the TOR must indicate the scope of decision-making authority and who employs it.

The project manager, unless functioning in some other (technical or client liaison) capacity, should only be required to visit at major milestones, when there is a requirement for a meeting with the client at the project or when something has gone wrong that requires a decision-making capacity, at the project site, beyond that of team members.

The project manager is best engaged in managing: absence of the project manager from the control centre creates opportunities for things to go wrong. It is tempting to believe that a 'hands-on' approach will increase the project manager's effectiveness but it may equally suggest that the team is less than adequate, unworthy of confidence. Monitoring visits may be the 'fun' part of project management but disabuse yourself of that notion; while the project manager is away the project will go astray.

The previous chart (Monitoring Schedule) can be expanded in subsequent editions of the plan of operation to develop the monitoring budget. In the example that follows (see next page), it is assumed that the salary cost of full-time staff is part of the on-going project cost; only consultant per day is calculated as additional to expenses.

> *A tragic and extreme example of the importance of monitoring in general terms can be seen in this extract from the Toronto Globe and Mail of August 25, 1997.*
>
> ### Why the Valujet disaster occurred.
>
> One hundred and ten people were killed when a Valujet DC-9 crashed in the Florida Everglades. The (US) National Transportation Safety Board inquiry, among other findings, stated:
>
> '...... the direct cause of the crash was a fire that had broken out among 144 improperly packed and transported oxygen containers. The fire resulted from a chain of serious operating and supervisory lapses on the part of Valujet, its maintenance contractor Sabretech and the Federal Aviation Administration.
>
> '....Sabretech itself subcontracted much of the maintenance work to unlicensed outside technicians, whose work it neglected to monitor properly. Valujet, in turn, failed to supervise the work Sabretech did on its behalf.'
>
> '.....the FAA failed to provide enough inspectors and to coordinate its inspections ....'
>
> In July 1999, the State of Florida charged Sabretech, the airline maintenance company, with murder and manslaughter. The company and three employees were later indicted by a federal grand jury for alleged conspiracy and the company for failure to train the personnel who handled the hazardous material. Later in 1999, the company alone was found guilty but had, of course, gone out of business.
>
> Hardly applicable to your average project you may say. True, but neglect of the basic principles causes the problems for projects and businesses of all sizes.

The need for adequate monitoring is a difficult concept to sell (I think I have said that before) and, when accepted, will still not be fully appreciated even upon successful project completion. It is always assumed in retrospect, that projects that succeed have had no problems. Equally, it is assumed (again, based on a successful project completion) that all the monitoring costs that were judged as unnecessary before commencement are **proven** unnecessary by the success of the project. This is one of the terrible crosses that the project manager has to bear – while smiling.

Project management may be 'incredibly easy' but monitoring, which is a major element, is incredibly undervalued and misunderstood.

Officer	Month 1 Site	Month 3 Factory	Month 4 Site	(Subsequent visits not shown)	Totals per officer
Project manager	time: 0 travel: 2200 meals: 280 lodging: 720 misc: 120 contin'cy: 332 total: **3652**				$ 3652
Agronomist	time: 2800 travel: 2200 meals: 280 lodging: 720 misc: 120 contin'cy: 612 total: **6732**		time: 2800 travel: 2200 meals: 280 lodging: 720 misc: 120 contin'cy: 612 total: **6732**		$ 13464
Procurement officer	time: 0 travel: 2200 meals: 280 lodging: 720 misc: 120 contin'cy: 332 total: **3652**	time: 0 travel: 800 meals: 140 lodging: 180 misc: 30 contin'cy: 115 total: **1265**			$ 4917
Procurement monitor	time: 2800 travel: 2200 meals: 280 lodging: 720 misc: 120 contin'cy: 612 total: **6732**	time: 1400 travel: 800 meals: 140 lodging: 180 misc: 30 contin'cy: 255 total: **2805**			$ 9537
Totals	20768	4070	6732		$ 31570

Assumed basic costs for the table above:

Consultant	$700.00	per day
Meals	$70.00	per day
Travel cost	$2,200.00	per journey (overseas)
Lodging	$180.00	per day
Travel cost	$800.00	per journey (home)
Misc.	$30.00	per day
Contingency	10%	

Although showing only a representative part of the monitoring for the previous hypothetical project at an overseas site (see page 187), it can be seen how quickly costs mount up, making assumptions based on costs prior to 2002. Nevertheless, the litany of horror stories of the consequences of the failure properly to monitor a project justifies adequate expenditure on monitoring of the project to ensure effective execution.

Better to spend adequately initially than risk both a project failure and a potentially disagreeable audit.

📖 *'Contracts, Terms of Reference'*

TAKE ANOTHER BREAK

7

Parameters

General

Cost, quality and time are the principal measuring factors that initially determine the planning limits and later, the progress and the success of a project. Each factor weighs differently with each client but it may be assumed that cost is more important to more clients than the others. The client will tell you, of course, that s/he is equally interested in quality but you must determine the reality and extent of this commitment for yourself, for each specific project, when it seems, as work progresses, that uncompromising adherence to quality parameters may jeopardise the budget or the schedule.

It is your obligation to give full consideration to all parameters at all times but you must also make a judgement of the true interests of the client and incline your recommendations in that direction. The client may not appreciate them as clearly as does the project manager; the client has imperatives and pressures, too, that cloud the vision and tend to suggest actions or conclusions that may not be in the long-term interests of the project. The project manager will be judged, when the project is completed, on actual results but his/her perceived performance during implementation of the project may prejudice the end result if the confidence of the client is lost. In other words, treat the matter of priorities delicately; do not hit the client over the head with an excess of reality. Suggestion and recommendation are more effective than contradiction. Everyone likes to be right all the time: the client is paying for that privilege but the onus is still on the project manger to complete the project within the established parameters. One other parameters is the conviction of having done a good job.

Woven within these basic project parameters are the nuances that both complicate and clarify their implementation. Milestones reduce project time to manageable elements; the work breakdown structure simplifies cost analysis and control; contingency allowances may seem to introduce an element of uncertainty but provide the flexibility required in uncertain cost environments; determination of the interfaces of all elements sharpens the project manager's perception of the magnitude and scope of each element and assists in their comprehensive description.

Cost

In respect of cost, the client is the one who funds the project and the client's interests are the first consideration. Do the client and yourself a favour by saving money as early as possible in the life of the project – it will be needed later. The best run projects more often than not tend to go over budget rather than under. There is a happy belief, fostered by both clients and consultants, that a cost overrun of 10% is permissible. I have even seen that written as a parameter. You may be sure that, given the option, the cost will increase.

📖 *'Parameters, Contingencies'*

Contingencies

Contingency considerations are never the same for any two projects; there is no such thing as a standard percentage contingency. It is not logical, reasonable or effective to add 10% to every project, indiscriminately. Fit the amount of the contingency to the special unknowns of each project and even to each part, stage, phase or element of a project.

As an example, if there are many potential variables of risk, develop a contingency related to schedule by tabulating the periods between milestones, determining the risk factor for each period and applying a contingency to each. It is normal that, as the implementation of the project proceeds, more uncertainties are resolved, therefore the risk factor is lessened; this should allow a reduction in the planned contingency for each consecutive phase of the work.

It is reasonable to suppose that initially, because of future unknowns, each subsequent work stage will incur an increasingly large percentage contingency before that stage is reached. When a stage is completed, the contingencies can be re-evaluated for all the subsequent stages as a degree of uncertainty will have been eliminated for the stages that follow. In addition, the poor performance of an early stage may clearly impact on or indicate a doubt about subsequent implementation performance that will cause you to increase the subsequent contingency allowances.

Alternatively, relate the contingency to the work breakdown structure. Calculate it either as a percentage or a lump sum but **based on all the information available at that time for that particular period or element**.

As the project progresses and a greater degree of certainty is attained, the unused contingency in completed periods or activities may be transferred forward, added to the budget for expansion of the mandate, or assumed to be no longer required and put back into the coffers.

There are mathematical formulas for these calculations (uncertainty and risk) but they are difficult to apply in the early stages of a project; the project manager's and the team's experience probably provide the most reliable guideline. The wise project manager will ensure that proper consideration is given to risk (however it be calculated) in all phases and that the accuracy of risk assessment and its relationship to contingency improves as the project progresses. It is better to err on the side of caution. Though large contingencies are usually frowned on by the client, your experience and acknowledgement by your client of that experience will give you the moral authority to make the necessary judgement and to convince the client.

A major element of cost and contingency calculation is the cost of monitoring and its effectiveness. Proper, early monitoring can improve the chances for reduction of contingencies in the later project stages. Accepting its value, its cost must be allowed for adequately at all stages and especially in planning.

'Communications, Charts – Organigram' for project control through money control and *'Monitoring, Budget'*; *'Parameters, Cost and Budget'*; *'Planning, Budget'*

Compromise

Determine as early as possible in the planning process where and what scales of compromise are allowed. When something has to give, know in advance what it is; time, cost or quality.

Depending on the viewpoint of the observer, this may be seen either as setting parameters for failure or setting them for success. In any event, every operation must be measurable in the terms mentioned (time, cost, quality) and if compromise is required, you must have established parameters indicating where cuts or changes may be made and how far they may go. These compromises are the end results of continuous monitoring and evaluation during project implementation.

You will find that most clients are reluctant to accept the possibility of a reduction in the scope of any of the parameters but especially disinclined to contemplate a cost overrun. To facilitate decision-making in respect of compromise, make sure there are detailed, measurable criteria (the more precise the better) in the planning documentation for all three parameters. Establishing and understanding these parameters during the planning stage may be more than a little depressing and have a negative effect on your perception of project success. Nevertheless, if this exercise leads you to a more realistic appreciation of the viability of the project, then it will not be a waste of time.

Also consider the possibility of **increases** in quality and **reduction** in completion time on the rare but happy occasion that the project performs better than anticipated. The same procedure applies as when contingency funds become available: plan for the possibility of **expanding** the mandate.

📖 *'Parameters, Cost and Budget'* and *'Parameters, Contingencies'*

Cost and budget

Project budget and project cost are not usually precisely the same thing. There are some institutional clients that become extremely upset should a project come in under budget. For most clients, of course, the opposite is true. But do not take the former lightly. An institutional executive whose budget is based on the previous year's spending, and who finds him/herself with a reduced departmental budget because a project cost less than s/he allotted, will not likely be a future client. As his/her budget often is set based on estimates by the project team and its staff or employed experts, then it is incumbent on the team to ensure that the estimate is as accurate as possible. Cost savings may be as unwelcome as cost overruns.

In a project, performed for this sort of institution, with many unknowns and consequent contingencies, it is always useful to plan peripheral or subsequent project elements that can absorb a funding surplus but which will have the dual potential of not jeopardising the project if they are not implemented but can be clearly shown to enhance the benefits already bestowed by the project, should they be effected. This should satisfy the client without prejudicing the integrity of the project manager's costing procedures.

There are clients who will view this procedure negatively but, in truth, they can hardly fail to benefit from it; it is largely a question of how the budget and contingencies are presented. For the client who simply wants to save money, then, do your best (fairly) to save money.

📖   *'Parameters, Contingencies'*

Interface

One of the most troublesome parameters that govern projects is the interface. It must be considered a parameter, and an important one, because it defines the coming together or the separation of many different conditions, people or elements. Failure carefully to seek out and define the interaction of these conditions or elements during project planning will surely lead to problems later. Some of the more obvious are described below.

Time

The beginning and end of a project are time interfaces; from zero (no activity) in project terms through the project duration to another zero when the project is complete. If nothing is happening prior to the project and then activities begin, we may consider this the first project interface. If there is no evaluation element, then completion of implementation is the final interface. Otherwise, that final point would be at the completion of evaluation and the completion/evaluation interface is a major milestone. Some projects, of course, carry extended warranties, giving another possible point of interface. See 'milestones' below.

Milestones

These may be considered either time, activity or phase/stage interfaces; they may also embrace physical elements. The completion of the walls of a building and the commencement of the roof have to occur to a time schedule and to specific physical stages of realisation; it is possible that different contractors undertake each stage of the work, giving the interface a contractual implication also.

A health project or programme with both educational and clinic construction elements (perhaps planned as two projects within the programme) could, as one example, interface at the milestone completion of the installation of equipment in the clinic and the milestone standard of training achieved within the educational element. This could be considered as both a time and a physical implementation interface as well as different but interacting milestones for each element and a major milestone for the total programme.

On multi-project programmes this can generate considerable complexity. It calls for meticulous planning and rigid monitoring. If physical and contractual milestones do not correspond as they should there is significant potential for contract delay claims and other costs.

Personnel

People interact with each other and their job descriptions require profound consideration of their interfaces. Any overlapping of descriptions or gaps that do not consider necessary contacts have the potential for serious problems. The interactions (interfaces) must be carefully described, either by job descriptions or by contracts or other agreements. Many of these interfaces will be obvious from the organigram for the project and, in more detail, from departmental or action unit organigrams. Although they may be immediately visible in an organigram, their importance merits a detailed description that will indicate what stimulates the interface, which person initiates or controls it, its anticipated results and the consequent activities.

📖 *'Responsibility, Job Description'*

Contracts

Theoretically, at least, they always start and finish and usually have points in **time or activity** that require interface with either other contractors or employees or client. From both the legal and practical point of view, an error in describing the conditions that surround such interfaces can be troublesome and costly in the extreme. Where there is coincidence between elements of two or more contracts, each contract should carry sufficient description to make clear the responsibility for **control** of the interface as well as the detail of the activities concerned. The description of the work of the contract, the scope of work, must provide for any element of doubt at these interfaces. Within a large project, the plan of operation will have considered these problems and will have brought them to the attention of the team in the 'strategy' description.

📖 *'Contracts, Scope of Work'*

Physical

Physical interfaces occur in construction, manufacturing and many other projects (are electronic interfaces 'physical'?). If two contractors are building towards the same point and either do not meet or, worse, pass each other, chaos is the result. It has happened that two sections of a spiral tunnel, started from both ends did not meet as they should. This is an easily understood circumstance (for the uninvolved observer) but is no more important than in the other applications mentioned nor in all the others you may think of.

Insurance

Insurance policies negotiated separately through contracts that are required to interface sometimes neglect either an important time or physical element that each thinks is the provenance of the other or of the client. An actual example: goods shipped overseas were covered on board ship and during transportation inland. Unfortunately, they were not insured while sitting on the dock. Where interfacing contracts are concerned and where they are all managed by an umbrella organisation (a project manager, for example), an insurance policy that covers all the concerned parties should be negotiated. This causes more than a few problems of complexity where different contracts terminate at different times but it can be done – it has been done. Find an insurer with this sort of experience.

Quality

This is the most difficult of the success parameters to define. In most cases, subjectivity is difficult to avoid, so the goal in applying quality as a measurement factor, should be to eliminate any doubt as to what is required **to the extent and detail possible**.

This means that all criteria that it is possible to measure should be stipulated in the plan of operation or some documentary annex of the plan. In construction projects, for example, there are norms or procedures established by most material manufacturers or suppliers; there are certain skill standards of trades and institutions, professional qualifications, bylaws and building codes. There are similar standards in other sciences. All these should be invoked and applied.

For other projects, try to apply the same principles. Such norms as exist should be cited. If there are none, the team must endeavour to apply some standards of achievement that will be acceptable to the client and useful to the team both in monitoring and evaluation. For example, a corn production project in a developing country might define quantity by tonnes per hectare and quality as acceptance and purchase by a recognised cooperative of 80% of the crop produced. While this may not be precise and is open to influence by other factors (a nationwide poor crop might make it acceptable even though of low quality), it sets a standard for determining the comparative success of the project.

Quality is equally important as a measurement parameter for a consultant contract and can be even more vexatious when trying to establish standards. Try to follow the same principles: it is better to have something measurable and it should be defined in terms that the consultant can appreciate before accepting the contract. One of the quality definitions for a report might be that certain conclusions be readily deduced from it to a standard of accuracy definable within a percentage range (plus or minus) of the eventual results that the report is instrumental in generating.

Some ingenuity is required in all cases that do not lend themselves to a physical measurement but it is better to establish something, imprecise though it may seem initially, rather than ignore the problem. If these standards are considered sufficiently early in the planning stage, development of the project plan may suddenly generate a dazzling insight that could solve or, at least, alleviate the problem.

A responsible consultant will take the care required to ensure that when his/her data is incorporated into the project it produces acceptable results. Certainly in the terms envisioned, it would be possible to determine after the event that it was a good report or good data – the skills required to determine this **before** applying the information must be assumed to be present in the team either by a specialist or by the team as a whole. Not easy!

📖 *'Contracts, Services, Consultants'*; *'Monitoring, Inspection'*

Time

General

Time is 'of the essence' both in contractual terms and in terms of project management effectiveness. It is critical that, from the beginning of planning to the completion of evaluation, all time be well expended. This manual places a great deal of emphasis on punctuality, on rapid approvals, on monitoring to avoid errors; there is the potential for time-wasting and procrastination at every stage of the project. The project manager who is not alert to effective use of time will not meet the deadlines. As a parameter, it is critical through all stages of a project and so finds itself addressed in several sections of this book.

📖 *'Contracts, Content'; 'Monitoring, Schedule'; 'Organisation, Punctuality'; 'Planning, Approvals'* and *'Time, Schedule'*

Approvals

Absolutely legitimate approvals required by the project management planning and implementation process have a substantial impact, often a critical impact, on the project time element. This requirement, both as a formal and an informal procedure, cannot be eliminated but it can be handled well or badly: turn to the Planning Section for more detail.

📖 *'Planning, Approvals'*

Punctuality

Expenditure of time that is not orderly, not precise and that does not contribute to the advancement of the project is not to be tolerated in the context of project management. At all times, be punctual yourself in all your project-related activities, persuade the team to be punctual, insist that your consultants and contractors be punctual and try to influence even your superiors to be punctual.

PUNCTUALITY

- *'Punctuality is the politeness of kings'.* – Louis XVIII

- *'Promptness tells me someone is more likely to be professional, respectful, reliable and considerate in our association'* – Eve Glicksman in the San Francisco Examiner

- The trouble with being punctual is that nobody else is there to appreciate it.

📖 *'Organisation, Punctuality'*

Schedule

Early team or group planning achieves cooperation that allows everyone (team members) to establish their **own** schedule; more often than not an optimistic one (do not let optimism overrule reason). Nevertheless, this is much more effective than forcing associates into a pre-established scheduling strait-jacket – and also lays a well-deserved guilt trip on them if they default.

Never conceal your true schedule from either the team or the client. Trying to apply pressure to the team by setting unrealistic completion targets is always ultimately counterproductive. Eventually the team's confidence in the project manager is undermined when the project inevitably falls behind a spurious schedule. Constantly redetermined target dates tend to lose their significance and are ignored even should they begin to approach the realistic. 'Slack time' is acceptable as a diminishing element of the schedule as the project proceeds but all the team should be aware of it; a proper spirit of cooperation within the team will encourage them not to dissipate it but, instead, to eliminate it and advance the project completion date.

Nor is there any point in concealing the true status of the project from the client. The project manager that knows what he or she is doing must be able to justify the schedule of future work and defend the activities of the past. It is better to include all performers in the planning/scheduling, to keep them informed of changes and to work with them to overcome any impediments that occur along the way.

'*Planning, Schedule*' and '*Planning, Approvals*'

Some final thoughts

- A belief in project management by 'consensus' (or anything else by consensus) is usually simply a rationalisation for not making decisions.

- 'Peer pressure' does not arise simply to make you do something you don't wish; more often it is the originator(s) of the pressure compensating for a weakness or insecurity in his or her own psyche.

- If a loophole exists someone will find and exploit it.

- When you begin your contribution to a project you necessarily accept what has preceded you unless you stipulate and record your reservations.

- Some dynamic managers are excellent at resolving a crisis. All too often they are the people who created the crisis. Dynamism is not the essential project management quality. Attention to detail, the monotonous stuff, is what forestalls the crisis in the first place. Mr. or Ms Plod has as good a chance (or better) of getting the job done properly.

- Any individual action is as likely to be motivated by a personal agenda as by a project agenda.

- Don't assume because a company or other legal entity, large or small, has been long established, has an enormous budget and a substantial management structure, that it knows what it is doing. If you have different ideas, you may be right!

- Successful project completion unfortunately appears to justify the idea that monitoring costs that were judged unnecessary on commencement are proven unnecessary by the success of the project!

- When reviewing a document or some other element of a project, it is easy to correct what is wrong but extraordinarily difficult to find what is missing. Make it easy by first creating your own 'model' as a yardstick (metre/meter-stick?) for assessment.

- It is equally easy to be unaware of that which is missing in a thing. So check the specification/description before you undertake an inspection: know what should be there.

- Behaving differently from other people may be assumed to indicate disapproval. This will be perceived as offensive – you may have to pay the price.

Appendix A
Logical Framework Analysis

The LFA is mentioned several times throughout this book. As a planning and monitoring tool it is unequalled in its simplicity. Its principal virtue is its clear exposition and arrangement of data. Being in the form of a chart on one sheet of paper, it lends itself to instant appraisal; the logic of the relationships between elements is apparent and it contains the fundamental evaluation criteria. For those not familiar with the method, an outline explanation follows.

Goal, Purpose, Outputs and Inputs are described in the 'Planning' section but, briefly, they are defined as follows:

Goal   The objective of the programme of which the project is a part; the long-term or overall objective.

Purpose   What the project should achieve; what the completion of the Outputs generates.

Outputs   The end results (usually physical) of the management of the Inputs.

Inputs   Resources of time, material, activities which, property managed, produce the Outputs.

The traditional arrangement of the columns within the table is shown below. Some of the terms or descriptions are variable but the principles remain the same.

NARRATIVE SUMMARY	OBJECTIVELY VERIFIABLE INDICATORS	MEANS OF VERIFICATION	IMPORTANT ASSUMPTIONS
Goal			
Purpose			
Outputs			
Inputs			

The project manager (PM) is specifically responsible for the first two levels of the vertical logic of the approach (Inputs and Outputs). The PM defines the Inputs that will provide the Outputs and is directly accountable for their control. In most organisations, a higher level of control (the Client – who may be a superior within your organisation) decides that the Outputs will produce the Purpose within the context of the Goal. *If the PM were also the planner, then he or she would have recommended both Purpose and Goal to the client. No matter what the circumstances, the PM might expect (or fear) to be blamed if the required Purpose does not result from even the most careful and proper management of the inputs and the provision of the Outputs.*

The vertical logic of the chart indicates the relationships between Input, Output, Purpose and Goal. If the right Inputs are provided and properly managed, then the Outputs will inevitably be produced; the same applies to the subsequent two levels.

Except that another inevitability is the tendency for things to go wrong. There are bound to be uncertainties – weather, strikes, soaring lending rates, shortage of competent personnel – all the things one cannot know with absolute assurance.

So, at every level, these uncertainties have to be considered and accounted for to the best of one's capacity in the context of experience and the information available at the time. Defining these uncertainties in the column 'Important Assumptions' does two things. In the planning stage it conditions the results of the Narrative Summary column at the next higher level in the chart. During implementation, it provides a warning that there are possible adverse circumstances of which the PM and the Team must be constantly aware and against which provision must be made.

For instance, a construction project (a worker's hostel, say) that is to commence under winter conditions might be substantially delayed by excessive frost. In such a case, it would be essential that this be considered and shown under 'Important Assumptions' as, perhaps, 'weather conditions suitable'. At a higher level, if the building is to house workers for an agricultural project, the Purpose (let us say, 'increase productivity at Farm 'X'') might be unachievable because the workers would not be available for the planting season. In this case, the Important Assumption at Output level is that 'the building be completed prior to commencement of planting season'. If the Output is not achieved to schedule and the Purpose is consequently foregone, so the achievability of the Goal will be jeopardised.

The two essential columns that define the logic of the approach are 'Narrative Summary' and 'Important Assumptions'. These must be correct (as far as possible) at each level in order to validate the Narrative Summary at the next level.

However, the second column, 'Objectively Verifiable Indicators' (OVI) are indispensable to rational judgement, indicating the type and magnitude of the things that enable you to measure the correctness of your project development criteria. The column 'Means of Verification' speaks for itself: these are your sources of information.

OVI permit you to break down the project into components of the magnitude that suits your convenience during the planning stage: they may be expanded or further broken down in your plan of operation or other planning documents. In the format of the LFA, it is easy to add to the listing as new elements are introduced and as new Important Assumptions force themselves on the attention. A hypothetical project is shown below: it is for the construction of worker accommodation on a farm, designed to provide labour where it was not readily available. All this is in the context of a national agricultural policy to increase productivity and the availability of produce.

NARRATIVE SUMMARY	OBJECTIVELY VERIFIABLE INDICATORS	MEANS OF VERIFICATION	IMPORTANT ASSUMPTIONS
GOAL contribute to improvement in national agricultural sector	Govt. incorporates production into national agricultural network	• annual Agricultural Department report • continuing monitoring reports	farm management properly utilises facilities and personnel
PURPOSE 1. improve worker availability 2. increase productivity at Farm X in current crop year	1. hostel 70% occupied at start of planting season 2. 100% increase over previous year's planting	• monitoring reports • farm management statistics	1. living environment acceptable to workers 2. suitable weather and work environment
OUTPUTS 1. workers' hostel (80 persons) 2. common family facilities	1. hostel complete 2. completed and equipped	• monitoring reports • construction completion documents	1. hostel available prior to planting season 2. completed and equipped at worker occupancy
INPUTS 1. government building loan 2. construction management 3. building site 4. construction contract	1. $1,000,000 at month 7 2. £200,00 at month 4 3. 0.5ha, no cost to project 4. $800,000 at month 7	1. Memo of Understanding 2. signed contract 3. agreement with farm authority 4. signed contract 5. monitoring of all elements	1. no change in Govt. financing policy 2. competent personnel available 3. suitable site available near Farm X 4. sufficient competitive bids

Note: this chart has been compressed into 4 columns to fit the page width.

Results

Simple logic permits a further step in the planning and analysis of projects. The provision of the Outputs consequent on certain activities applied to the inputs (or inherent in the provision of the inputs) gives certain definable results which are more susceptible of interpretation than simple Outputs and Purpose; perhaps a certain amount of subjectivity is required to develop the correct interpretation. In the example given, a result could be 'workers functioning effectively in a family environment that makes working in this area acceptable' This particular 'result' will be induced by behavioural changes in the subjects of the project because of the provision of the Outputs; all of which make the achievement of the Purpose possible. The degree of subjectivity in the analysis of achievement in this case is in the significance of the word 'functioning'; are the workers just putting in time or are they better, happier, more efficient workers because of the Outputs? In the latter optimistic case, more workers will be happy to be employed there and that will most likely lead to an increase in productivity. Measuring 'happiness' is no easy task but everything is susceptible of evaluation if it or its consequences is/are broken down into sufficient elements.

'Results' will be apparent to some extent in the realisation of the Purpose, which has simple, objectively measurable indicators. A revised LFA, including 'Results', is shown opposite. Potential subjectivity in the analysis of achievement tends to invalidate the middle two columns which may well be ignored.

A more graphic illustration of the introduction of 'Results' is the sequence of events as shown on page 208. The traditional LFA sequence is shown in bold-face on the left and 'Results' are introduced into the sequence as previously shown in the LFA chart opposite. The rationale illustrated in the diagram is that 'operational activities' or other tangible, concrete applications of the Outputs generate a Result or Results. In a similar way, having achieved the Purpose, an impact will be made on the socioeconomic environment to complement other activities that lead to the achievement of the Goal.

NARRATIVE SUMMARY	OBJECTIVELY VERIFIABLE INDICATORS	MEANS OF VERIFICATION	IMPORTANT ASSUMPTIONS
GOAL contribute to improvement in national agricultural sector	Govt. incorporates production into national agricultural network	● annual Agricultural Department report ● continuing monitoring reports	other elements of National Plan fully complement this one
RESULTS workers remain productively employed in salubrious family environment	*develop detailed criteria for analysis of conditions obtaining in continuing operations*	● *evaluation and subsequent reviews*	farm management properly uses facilities and personnel
PURPOSE 1. improve worker availability 2. increase productivity at Farm X in current crop year	1. hostel 70% occupied at start of planting season 2. 100% increase over previous year's planting	● monitoring reports ● farm management statistics	1. living environment acceptable to workers 2. suitable weather and work environment
RESULTS 1. workers functioning effectively in a family environment	*develop detailed criteria for analysis of circumstances obtaining in operational mode*	● *special monitoring mission*	1. working and living environment acceptable to farm staff
OUTPUTS 1. workers' hostel (80 persons) 2. common family facilities	1. hostel complete 2. completed and equipped	● monitoring reports ● construction completion documents	1. hostel available prior to planting season 2. completed and equipped at worker occupancy
INPUTS 1. government building loan 2. construction management 3. building site 4. construction contract	1. $1,000,000 at month 7 2. £200,00 at month 4 3. 0.5ha, no cost to project 4. $800,000 at month 7	1. Memo of Understanding 2. signed contract 3. agreement with farm authority 4. signed contract 5. monitoring of all elements	1. no change in Govt. financing policy 2. competent personnel available 3. suitable site available near Farm X 4. sufficient competitive bids

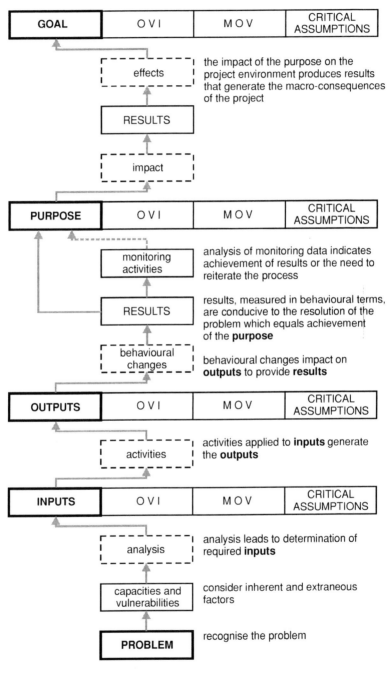

| GOAL | O V I | M O V | CRITICAL ASSUMPTIONS |

effects

the impact of the purpose on the project environment produces results that generate the macro-consequences of the project

RESULTS

impact

| PURPOSE | O V I | M O V | CRITICAL ASSUMPTIONS |

monitoring activities

analysis of monitoring data indicates achievement of results or the need to reiterate the process

RESULTS

results, measured in behavioural terms, are conducive to the resolution of the problem which equals achievement of the **purpose**

behavioural changes

behavioural changes impact on **outputs** to provide **results**

| OUTPUTS | O V I | M O V | CRITICAL ASSUMPTIONS |

activities

activities applied to **inputs** generate the **outputs**

| INPUTS | O V I | M O V | CRITICAL ASSUMPTIONS |

analysis

analysis leads to determination of required **inputs**

capacities and vulnerabilities

consider inherent and extraneous factors

PROBLEM

recognise the problem

Appendix B

Articles of Agreement

A contract between a Client and a Consultant may be as complex a document as you care to make it or so simple as to be useless; or anything in between. The reader may consider the example that follows as unnecessarily detailed. I do not think so. If you want to make sure that the work is well done and that it provides the information or other services that you want, then several things are required:

- a descriptive statement that embraces the generality of the work (grandparent clause)
- a complete detailed description of the work
- divisions of the work that can be monitored and evaluated as work proceeds
- a fee structure that lends itself to payment according to items of work performed
- the clearest possible indication of the quality of the work required
- a warranty that obligates the consultant to perform well
- some methodology for terminating the contract in a manner fair to both parties
- a time schedule for the performance of the work
- and other conditions contained in the Agreement that follows.

There is no doubt that many of the contingencies anticipated by such a contract will not occur (it is too awful to contemplate every contingency arising). One of the best assurances of avoiding any unpleasantness between the parties is to make sure that as many loopholes as possible have been closed and that both the Client and the Consultant have a thorough understanding of what each party is to provide. I am especially concerned that many clients do not take the trouble to break down the consultant's work into pieces that can be assessed during the progress of the work. The following document is a base for such an agreement; it is neither necessarily complete nor applicable to your special needs. Still, it is more substantial than most consultant contracts. This example shows the work in measurable units that can be reimbursed as they are satisfactorily completed. But don't forget – make sure your lawyer has read and agreed to any contract before you sign it. **This manual is not meant to be a legal brief.**

ARTICLES OF AGREEMENT

THESE ARTICLES OF AGREEMENT ARE MADE AS OF THE ___ **day of** ___ **20**___

BETWEEN: The Metropolis International Institute, hereinafter referred to as the CLIENT, OF THE FIRST PART,

AND: Fred Bloggs, hereinafter referred to as the CONSULTANT, OF THE SECOND PART.

WHEREAS the Client is to (brief description of the work) at (the location if applicable), and

WHEREAS the Consultant, in consideration of the payment and in accordance with the conditions specified herein, has undertaken to perform those services described in the **Description of the Work**.

THEREFORE, the CLIENT and the CONSULTANT agree as follows:

AI   CONTRACT

AI .1   The following documents and any amendments relating thereto form the contract between the Client and the Consultant:

AI .1.1   these Articles of Agreement;

AI .1.2   the document attached hereto entitled General Conditions;

AI .1.3   the document attached hereto entitled Description of the Work;

AI .1.4   the document attached hereto entitled Terms of Payment;

AI .1.5   any amendment hereto agreed by the parties in writing.

AI .2   In the event of discrepancies, inconsistencies or ambiguities in the wording of these documents, the document first appearing shall rule over those subsequently listed.

A2   COMPLETION

A2.I   The Consultant shall commence the work immediately following the signing of this Agreement and conclude all items to the complete satisfaction of the Client, within ____ calendar weeks *(days/months/ years)* except as may be otherwise agreed within the terms and conditions of this contract.

A3   CONTRACT AMOUNT

A3. 1   Subject to the terms and conditions of this contract and in consideration of the performance of the services, the Client shall pay to the Consultant the sum of _____ Pounds Sterling (£____) (or other currency)

A4   CONTRACT LAW

A4.l   This contract shall be governed and construed by the laws of the *(country, province, state, or other jurisdiction).*

A5   CLIENT'S REPRESENTATIVE

A5.l   For the purposes of this contract the Client shall be represented by

_____

A6   COMMUNICATiONS

A6.l   All communications between the parties or their representatives shall be deemed to have been received by the addressee if delivered by mail as follows:

     to the Client at : (mailing address)

     to the Consultant at: (mailing address)

A7   SUCCESSION

A7.l   The Contract shall enure to the benefit of and be binding upon the parties hereto, their respective heirs, legal representatives, successors and assigns.

A7.2   In witness whereof the parties have executed this Agreement in two originals under their respective corporate seals and by the hands of their duly authorised officers.

SIGNED, SEALED AND DELIVERED

Client _____ Consultant _____

Executive Director _____

          ....

GENERAL CONDITIONS

Consulting Services

GC1   INTERPRETATION   In this Contract:

GC1 .1   'contract' means the contract documents referred to in the Articles of Agreement;

GC1 .2   'services' or 'work', unless otherwise expressed in the contract, means everything that is necessary to be done, supplied or delivered by the Consultant to perform his/her obligations under the contract;

GC1 .3 'Client's Representative' means the officer or employee of the Client who is designated by the Articles of Agreement and includes any person designated by the Client's Representative to perform any of his/her functions under the contract;

GC1 .4 'Consultant' means *(name of Consultant or firm)*

GC2 ASSIGNMENT

GC2.I Neither party to the contract shall assign the contract or any portion thereof without the written consent of the other, which consent shall not be unreasonably withheld.

GC3 ARBITRATION

GC3.I In the event of a dispute between the parties as to their respective rights and obligations under the Contract, either party shall give notice to the other within 30 days of the occurrence of the dispute. Within 10 days of said notice, the Client and the Consultant shall each nominate an arbitrator. A third arbitrator shall be jointly nominated by the first two. Failing agreement on a third arbitrator, a request shall be made to the *(here name some independent body in whom both parties trust and who is willing to act – or perhaps a party that has an independent interest in the work)* to provide the services of an officer to act as arbitrator.

GC3.2 The unanimous decisions of the arbitrators shall be rendered within 30 days of their appointment and shall be binding on both parties to the contract.

GC4 INDEMNIFICATION

GC4.I The Client indemnifies the Consultant and holds him/her harmless from all claims, actions demands, suits, losses or proceedings arising out of or attributable to a negligent act or omission of the Client or his other consultants or contractors.

GC4.2 The Consultant accepts full responsibility for costs or damages that may result from errors ineluctably attributable to project design *(or other professional expertise – change accordingly)* criteria or development by the Consultant, his partners, employees, sub-consultants or associates that the Client cannot reasonably be expected to have approved or accepted by want of the specific knowledge or experience in which the Consultant is acknowledged as pre-eminent.

GC5 WORK UNITS & SUSPENSION

GC5.1 The work comprises four (4) *(or as agreed – change accordingly)* units as described in the Description of the Work.

GC5.2   The Client may, by prior agreement and without prejudice to the rights or other recourse of either party, suspend the contract at the completion of any of the units. However, the Client undertakes that no other consultant shall be employed to complete the subsequent contracted units at anytime, other than the Consultant, party to this Contract, except as may otherwise be determined under clause GC6. 1, paragraphs a) to d) of these General Conditions.

GC5.3   In the event of reinstatement of the project, the Client and the Consultant agree to negotiate in good faith a new fee structure for the completion of the work within the terms established in this contract.

GC6   TERMINATION OF THE CONTRACT BY THE CLIENT

GC6.I   The Client may, without prejudice to any other right or remedy he may have, give the Consultant written notification of the postponement or termination of the Contract if the Consultant:

    a) should be adjudged bankrupt;

    b) refuse or neglect to provide sufficient and proper employees, services and logistical support to perform the work;

    c) disregard laws or regulations of authorities having jurisdiction over the work;

    d) otherwise violate the provisions of the Contract to a substantial degree.

    e) or if circumstances beyond the control of the Client warrant a discontinuance or postponement of the project.

GC6.2   Should the Client terminate the Contract under the conditions indicated above, the Consultant shall be entitled to be paid promptly for all work properly completed to the date of receipt of notice of the termination.

GC7   TERMINATION OF THE CONTRACT BY THE CONSULTANT

GC7.I   The Consultant may, without prejudice to any other right or remedy he may have, give the Client written notification of the termination of the Contract if the Client:

    a) should be adjudged bankrupt;

    b) should stop or otherwise delay the work for a period in excess of thirty *(30 – change to suit)* days, provided such delay is not due to default of the Consultant;

    c) not make payment in accordance with the terms of this contract.

GC8   CONFLICT OF INTEREST

GC8.I   The Consultant declares that he/she has no pecuniary interest in the business of any third party that could cause a conflict of interest in carrying out the work. Should such an interest be assumed during the life of the Contract, the Consultant shall declare it to the Client's Representative.

GC9 CONSULTANT WARRANTY

GC9.I   The Consultant warrants that he/she is competent to perform the services required under this Contract in that he/she has the necessary knowledge, skill, training, available time and resources to perform the services.

GC9.2   The Consultant undertakes to perform the work with all due care, diligence and skill to the complete satisfaction of the Client.

GC1O PUBLICITY

GC1O.I   This Contract and the work it governs shall be considered confidential between the parties to the Contract and neither the contract nor the work nor any of their parts shall be used in publicity matter in any medium without prior permission of the Client.

GC11 ENTIRE AGREEMENT

GC11.1   This Contract constitutes the entire agreement between the parties with respect to the subject matter of the Contract and supersedes all previous negotiations, communications and other agreements relating to it unless they be included in the Contract.

D DESCRIPTION OF THE WORK

DI .0 RESPONSIBILITIES

DI .1   In order to complete the Work to the full satisfaction of the Client, the consultant shall obtain all information that will govern the work, produce the work within the parameters outlined below, while ensuring conformance with all applicable regulations, and obtain the necessary approvals of authorities having jurisdiction that may be required to complete the work.

DI.2   The Work comprises everything required to produce _____ *(description)* and shall include the following:

a. obtain from whatever source all relevant information and documentation required to complete the Work,

b. study this documentation and, within the Client's development criteria and applicable regulations, produce a _____ *(describe)* to the Client's approval;

c. establish a schedule of production to the approval of the Client and conform to this schedule at all times; the schedule shall indicate commencement of the Work, proposed completion of the various stages (see below), anticipated unofficial and official submissions to the authorities having jurisdiction, requirements for approval by the Client and the proposed completion of the Work;

d. cooperate with the authorities having jurisdiction at various stages of the Work in order to ensure the most rapid completion of the Work;

e. liaise with the Client or his representative to obtain approvals during production of the Work, giving at least 7 days notice to the Client of any requirement for his approval;

f. develop a _____ *(describe special details)*

g. perform all the Work to relevant _____ *(describe)* regulations.

D2   WORK STAGES

D2.1   Approvals will be required of the Client at the following stages:

a   Preliminary   *(describe)*

b.   Preliminary   *(describe as applicable)*

c.   Intermediate   *(describe as applicable)*

d.   Any intermediate stages due to required changes by authorities having jurisdiction

e.   Final draft documents

f.   Final completed documents

D3   DOCUMENTATION REQUIRED

D3.I   The following materials comprise the documentation to be provided by the consultant as part of the Work:

a   *(describe)*

b   *(describe)*

c   *(describe)*

d   *(describe)*

D4   SPECIAL PARAMETERS

D4.1   The Client has certain requirements which shall be included in the Work except in so far as they may conflict with requirements and regulations established by the authorities having jurisdiction, in which case the latter shall rule.

D4.2   The Client's requirements are:

a   *(describe)*

b *(describe)*

c *(describe)*

D5 UNITS OF WORK

D5.I The work consists of four (4) units as follows:

Unit 1 – *(describe)*

Unit 2 – *(describe)*

Unit 3 – *(describe)*

Unit 4 – *(describe)*

D6 SCHEDULE OF ACTIVITIES

D6.I All work shall be completed by the indicated final date of the agreed and initialled schedule, except as this date may be modified by mutual agreement of the parties within the terms of this Contract.

D6.2 The Consultant shall perform the work in a timely manner and submit documents for approval in accordance with the agreed schedule of activities. However, it is expressly agreed by the Client that the Consultant shall not be held responsible for any delay caused by failure of the Client to provide scheduled decisions as required or by any act of another Client-employed consultant or contractor.

D6.3 Any request for extension of time due to delay caused by others must be notified immediately in writing by the Consultant and, if agreed by the Client, shall be incorporated into the schedule.

TERMS OF PAYMENT

TP1 BASIS OF PAYMENT

TP1 .1 For the performance, to the Client's satisfaction, of the services described in the Description of the Work, the Client covenants and agrees to pay the Consultant on the following basis:

TP1 .2 The total fee for the services described in the Description of the Work shall be as indicated in the Articles of Agreement (Contract Amount).

TP1 .3 The schedule of payment of the total fee follows:

All Units

a) upon signing this Agreement _____ £ _____

Unit 1

a) (describe) _____ £ _____

b) (describe) _____ £ _____

Unit 2

a) (describe) _____ £ _____

b) (describe) _____ £ _____

Unit 3

a) (describe) _____ £ _____

b) (describe) _____ £ _____

Unit 4

a) (describe) _____ £ _____

b) (describe) _____ £ _____

TOTAL FEE £ _____

All the above amounts are due and payable on completion of the work to the complete satisfaction of the Client.

TP1 .4   The Client may request additional services or they may be required due to changes of scope originated by the Client. Charges for such additional services shall be made on the basis of actual and reasonable expenditure of staff time at the following rates, all-inclusive of overheads and profit (but not including expenditures that are reimbursed separately under this contract) as follows:

	Daily
Senior Consultant	£ _____
Consultant	£ _____
Technician	£ _____

TP2   METHOD OF PAYMENT

TP2.I   Except in the case of the first payment when no notice shall be required, the Consultant shall give the Client ten (10) days written notice of the intention to submit an invoice for payment in accordance with the terms of the Basis of Payment. The invoice shall be submitted in two (2) copies.

TP2.2   Prior to receipt of the invoice, Representatives of the Consultant and the Client shall meet to undertake reviews and/or inspections to determine that the work to be claimed for has, in fact, been performed to the satisfaction of the Client.

TP2.3   Payment of approved invoices shall be made by the Client within thirty (30) calendar days of the date of the invoice by cheque to the Consultant's address of record.

TP2.4   Any due payment not received by the Consultant within forty-five (45) days of the invoice date, when the invoice has been properly despatched, shall be considered past due and the consultant shall be entitled to interest on the due amount at an annual interest rate equal to that of the *(name of bank)* on the last day the invoice was due plus one and a half percent.

TP2.5   The Consultant shall provide official receipts for all amounts immediately upon receipt of payment.

Appendix C

Application for Funding

You may find this document useful as a legal vehicle appropriate to the granting of funds, previously applied for, for the performance of a service or the supply of goods. It was designed originally for use by a Non-Governmental Organisation (NGO), acting as an Executing Agency for a government donor department. The objective was to co-fund projects performed by smaller NGOs through an administrative intermediary.

LETTER OF AGREEMENT

Date _____   File No _____

To _____

Subject: Agreement between _____ *(recipient)* and _____ *(name of executing agency)*

Project Title _____

Date of Agreement _____

I am pleased to inform you that the *(executing agency)* has agreed to finance the above-referenced project from the *(source of funds)* budget, sponsored by the *(Government Department)*. This letter, the attached Annexes and any mutually agreed amendments to them comprise the entire Agreement between your organisation and the *(executing agency)*.

Annex A to the Agreement is the Terms and Conditions governing the Agreement; Annex B is a description of the project; Annex C is the detailed budget and disbursement schedule. In the case of any discrepancy, omission or any inconsistency between the documents, the one first appearing (including this letter) shall rule over those following.

As the Implementing Agency for this project, responsible for its successful completion and for the proper disbursement of the matching funds, we ask that you read these conditions and, if you agree with them, return a signed copy of the Letter of Agreement and initialled copies of each page of the Annexes to the Palestine Council of Health.

Yours truly,

_____ Programme Manager

I have read and agree to the terms and conditions specified in this letter and the attached Annexes, A, B, and C.

Name _____

Signature _____ Date _____

Title _____

Organisation _____

Responsible Officer _____ Telephone _____

TERMS AND CONDITIONS of the AGREEMENT

1. The Implementing Agency (Agency) shall commence work immediately on the project as described in Annex B and shall complete the work in accordance with the schedule established in Annex C or as shall be subsequently agreed between the parties.

2. Subject to conformity with the terms and conditions of this Agreement, including the financial and reporting requirements, *(name of Executing Agency or source of funds)*, on behalf of the *(funding agency)*, shall disburse to the Agency a total amount of _____ (£ _____)

3. This Agreement shall be governed and construed by the laws of the *(Province, state or other legal jurisdiction)*

4. For the purposes of this Agreement, the Executing Agency shall be represented by: _____

   and the Agency by _____

5. All communications between the parties or their representatives shall be deemed to have been received by the addressee if delivered by mail as follows:

   to The Executing Agency at the following address:

   _____

   to the Agency at:

   _____

6. In the event of a dispute between the parties as to their respective rights and obligations under the Agreement, either party shall give notice to the other within 15 days of the occurrence of the dispute. Within 10 days of the said

notice, The Executing Agency and the Agency shall each nominate a representative to resolve the dispute. The two representatives jointly shall request the *(choose an uninvolved organisation of substantial reputation that would be prepared to act as an arbitrator)* to nominate a third representative to assist in deciding the dispute.

7   Decisions of the committee of three shall be rendered unanimously within 30 days of the appointment of the *(outside agency or organisation)* representative and shall be binding on both parties to the Agreement.

8   The Implementing Agency indemnifies The Executing Agency and holds the Executing Agency and the Funding Agency harmless from all claims, actions, demands, suits, losses or proceedings arising out of or attributable to a negligent act or omission of the Agency or the Agency's affiliates, coalition members, consultants, contractors, suppliers or other dependents of the Agency.

9   The Executing Agency may, without prejudice to any other right or remedy it may have, give the Agency written notification of the postponement or termination of the Agreement if the Agency should:

   a) be adjudged bankrupt;

   b) refuse or neglect to furnish reports and accounts as provided for in this Agreement;

   c) otherwise violate the provisions of the Agreement to a substantial degree;

   d) should the transfer of authorised funds to IDP be unduly delayed or cancelled by the *(source of funds)*.

10   The Agency may, without prejudice to any other right or remedy it may have, give The Executing Agency written notification of the postponement or termination of the Agreement if the Executing Agency should:

   a) be adjudged bankrupt;

   b) refuse or delay disbursements more than 30 days beyond their due date, provided such delay is not due to default of the Agency;

   c) otherwise violate the provisions of the Agreement to a substantial degree.

11   The Agency also agrees:

   a) to sponsor, support and manage the project under the terms and conditions outlined in the request for co-funding and as recommended and/or modified by the Program Committee and ratified by the Executing Agency and in accordance with this Agreement;

b) to use the funds disbursed by The Executing Agency from the *(source of funds)* in support of the budget of the Agency's project described in Annex B. The budget and disbursement schedule which is attached as Annex C forms an integral part of this Agreement and is a specific commitment by the Agency to disburse the amounts indicated;

c) to inform The Executing Agency in writing, in advance, and in a timely manner, of all significant modifications to the project implementation and of any budget change of a magnitude of approximately twenty percent (20%) of the total budget amount;

d) to return to the Executing Agency any funds disbursed from the *(source of funds)* which were not transferred or accounted for in accordance with the terms of this Agreement and as were recommended by the Fund Committee, taking into account the agreed matching fund ratio;

e) to maintain such accounting records that the funds administered for the project, including disbursements against the funds received, may be clearly identified and verified; originals of these records, documents and statements shall be retained by the Agency for a minimum period of five years following mutually agreed completion of the project;

f) to prepare and submit to the Executing Agency both interim and final implementation and finance reports according to the reporting schedule in Annex C. The reports shall outline the actual results achieved, relative to the goals and objectives detailed in the submission, for the period ending on the report date with a cumulative schedule of advances received and (in the case of an interim report) of anticipated future disbursements. Each report shall be signed by the Agency Representative or an authorised delegate;

g) to provide, for financial or operational purposes, at the request of the Executing Agency or its authorised representative, all relevant records, documents and statements under the control of the Agency pertaining to the project; all receipts and cancelled cheques as well as customs documents, bills of lading and other relevant documentation in respect of goods purchased in *(country/state)* or elsewhere and transferred to the project;

h) to ensure that any and all accrued interests earned on the funds be used for the same purposes as the principal amount and that the interests be accounted for in the same manner. Interests earned that are not disbursed as described, prior to the agreed completion of the project, shall be returned to *(the source of funds)* through the Executing Agency in the three months following the completion of the project and the submission and acceptance of the final report;

I) to send official receipts to the Executing Agency for all funds transferred to the Agency by the Executing Agency be it by cheque or other financial instrument within three days of receipt of the funds;

j) to send copies of bank drafts or cancelled cashed cheques or other recognised instruments to the Executing Agency as proof that all project funds have been transferred to the project partner in the field according to the disbursement schedule submitted;

k) to match the IDP disbursement with the Agency's contribution as outlined in the Agency's request and as subsequently recommended by the Program Committee and indicated in the budget attached as Annex C;

l) to acknowledge the support provided by *(source of funds)*, through the Executing Agency, and by the Executing Agency in the Agency's annual financial statements, annual reports, speeches, press releases, publications and other material;

m) to cooperate to the extent required to permit review and evaluation of projects as required by the Executing Agency and to require the same of Partners, and dependents of the Agency.

12   the Executing Agency shall:

a) make a first payment to the Agency in accordance with the payment schedule outlined in Annex C of this Agreement, subject always to the previous approval and transfer of funds by the source of funds;

b) make further payments in accordance with the payment schedule outlined in Annex C subject always to the timely receipt of satisfactory implementation and financial reports stipulated in Annex C and subject always to the approval of funds by the source of funds.

13   Terms used in this Agreement are defined as follows:

a) 'Agreement' means all those documents referred to in the Letter of Agreement;

b) 'project', unless otherwise expressed in the Agreement, means everything that is necessary to be done, supplied, or delivered by the Agency in order to complete the Agency's obligations under the Agreement and to achieve the objectives described in Annex B of the Agreement;

c) 'Executing Agency' means the officer or employee of the Executing Agency Health who is designated by the Terms and Conditions of this Agreement and includes any person nominated by the Executing Agency Representative to perform the Executing Agency's obligations under the Agreement;

d) 'Agency' means the Implementing Agency, party with the Executing

Agency to this Agreement;

e) 'Agency Representative' means the officer or employee of the Agency who is designated by the Terms and Conditions of this Agreement and includes any person nominated by the Agency Representative to perform the Agency obligations under the Agreement.

Note to reader: *The Application for Co-funding or Proposal can serve as the Annex B (description of the project). The budget and schedule of implementation (or amendments required by the Program Committee) can serve as Annex C.*

Appendix D

Coalition Agreement

There are times when two or more organisations (for example, Non-Governmental Organisations – NGOs) may wish to cooperate in the implementation of a project. The difficulty in such a case is apportioning responsibility for performance of the work and especially so should things go wrong. Turning back to the Section on Charts and Diagrams, you will see that responsibility cannot easily be shared. In the case of a coalition such as the one suggested, it is logical and easy to make one of the members of the coalition primarily responsible to the funding body. This provides a line of command and saves the Executing Agency the thankless task of arbitrating between members of a group whose initial enthusiastic cooperation may have turned to acrimony. I repeat the caution that one should always have a lawyer review the document in the proper context of the other agreements that may limit this one. This particular example could be attached to a co-funding application as an Annex

ANNEX
TERMS AND CONDITIONS OF A COALITION AGREEMENT

LETTER OF AGREEMENT

Date _____ File No _____

To: The Executive Director,

       International Development Program Secretariat

Dear Sir or Madam:

   Subject: Agreement between:

_____ (the Lead Agency) and

_____ (a Support Agency) and

_____ (a Support Agency)

   Project Title _____

   Date of Agreement _____

We the above-named duly registered Non-Government Organisations (Agencies)

have agreed to cooperate in the implementation of the referenced project, co-funded by the International Development Program (IDP).

We do hereby agree both among ourselves and with the Executing Agency (International Development Program Secretariat) to the following:

a) each and all members of the Coalition conform to the eligibility requirements of the Executing Agency relative to the procedures of the IDP, and accordingly attach the necessary supporting documentation as indicated in the IDP Procedures Manual;

b) the nominated Lead Agency shall sign a Letter of Agreement with the Executing Agency of which the terms and conditions and applicable Annexes shall have equal force and be binding on each and all of the members of this Coalition of Agencies in respect of their special obligations under this Agreement as indicated in the required 'responsibility matrix' (see below);

c) on behalf of the Coalition Members, the Lead Agency accepts full responsibility for the proper completion of the project and the members of the Coalition freely accept the pre-eminence of the Lead Agency and agree to be bound by all the terms and conditions of its Agreement with the Executing Agency;

d) the attached responsibility matrix is a true indication of the work that shall be performed by each member of the coalition in respect of the implementation of the project and each member hereby undertakes to perform such activities in accordance with the schedule submitted by the Lead Agency and previously agreed between all members of the coalition and within the context of the Agreement between the Lead Agency and the Executing Agency;

e) any proposed change to this Agreement shall be notified to the Executing Agency by the Lead Agency, in a timely manner and no change shall be made without the prior approval of the Executing Agency;

f) this Agreement is duly executed by a suitably authorised officer of each of the members of the Coalition.

Signed _____

   for _____ (the Lead Agency)

Signed _____

   for _____ (the Support Agency)

Signed _____

   for _____ (the Support Agency)

Appendix E
Work Breakdown Structure

Work Breakdown Structures for different sectors can vary enormously in detail but not in principle. The logical thought process is the same for the development of an aid project or for a referendum as it is for a construction project. Because we all know a little about building, I use that as an example – it is also a lot easier for me!

The WBS that follows is for a typical domestic residence and is based on the premise of sub-contracting the work by trades. 'Drywall, for example, is gypsum wall board (GWB) and includes application and fixing by screw or nail, taping, filling and sanding and usually presumes the previous installation of insulation and vapour barrier. All trades may not have been included in the chart but it is of no consequence to the sequence of the breakdown shown in the chart.

Note that 'Services' is one sub-contract, broken down at the next level into 'Plumbing' and 'Electrical'. The assumption in this WBS is that you have selected your services contractor as one who does both mechanical and electrical work. You may ask that sub-contractor to split the work into the two main trades and even ask for a further sub-division as, for instance, 'rough and finish', 'heating', and 'light fixtures' all being included in the 'electrical' trade or activity. Now you have the opportunity, should you need it, to make changes (or the Client has that opportunity) to any of the three electrical sub-activities in the full knowledge of how that change would affect the total stipulated price of the contract.

If the Client decides to use gas heating, the electrical heating is shown at level 4 as an isolated amount and can be eliminated from the electrical contract. Because you have selected a contractor that does a total mechanical and electrical service, you can request a new price for a gas installation and incorporate it into the WBS, affecting only the cost of 'services' at level 2 and, of course, the total stipulated price of 'House' at level 1. Alternatively, you may call another sub-trade to tender for the gas heating.

The detail for the activity (sub-trade) 'Paint' is typical for all the sub-trade contracts. In this case, a contingency of 8% has been applied to the cost. This is because, although you know that your contractor is prompt, an excellent worker, that he always keeps to schedule and returns for touching up, nevertheless, he tends to be untidy and you have increased costs for clean-up. Were it an unknown painter, you might have to increase the contingency to 12% or 15% because a painter can make or break a project and you may have to follow a poor performer with your own touch-up or painting crew for which you need extra money. Theoretically, you may back-charge a sub-trade for sloppy work. A tough and well-organised project manager will have smaller contingencies than most.

Of course, you may not actually draw a WBS with little boxes such as the one for 'Paint'. If you are using a computer spreadsheet or other program, all that information will be fed into the machine. Again, you may simply put all the data onto individual estimating sheets and refer to the sheets on your WBS diagram. If you have a good imagination, you may not need the diagram. However, I am sure that, in most cases you will find that it simplifies the work enormously. The important thing is to appreciate the logic of the breakdown and to use it in conjunction with estimating, organisation, interfacing, scheduling and contracting.

Referring, in this book, to 'Planning, Work Breakdown Structure'; it can be seen that 'House' may readily be replaced by 'Develop Aid Program'. On the second level we might have 'Establish Management Structure', 'Seek Government Cooperation' and 'Fund-Raising'. This latter (for example) would go to level three as four tasks, 'fund-raising plan', 'solicit volunteers', 'print circulars' and 'television advertising'. Each of these would break down to a fourth level and thus develop a series of activities against which one could put a cost (budget preparation) and which would, amongst other things, provide information for the development of an organigram.

WORK BREAKDOWN STRUCTURE

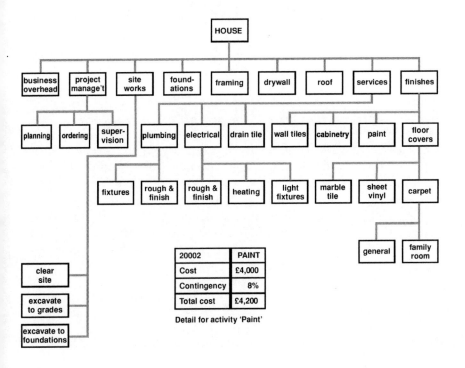

20002	PAINT
Cost	£4,000
Contingency	8%
Total cost	£4,200

Detail for activity 'Paint'

Other management books
by Norman Willoughby

Project Management for Builders and Contractors

Over 50 years experience in management, construction, development and design has been distilled by the author into a practical, perceptive handbook, useful to everyone involved at any stage of the building process. There are suggestions on building practice for the builder or contractor who wishes to improve both performance and profit by adopting the essential elements of project management methods. Vancouver Island's Business Examiner described it as 'a how-to manual for both small and large contractors, with an eye to good organising and profit.'

ISBN 0-9698126-1-2 Canada $29.95   US $22.95

We Always Do It That Way – *fearless revolution management*

At last, an approach to the hazards of home improvements told as a comedy of errors but with a host of practical tips and sample documents that will help the homeowner deal with the mysteries and potential horrors of renovations and additions.

ISBN 0-9698126-2-0   Canada $19.95   US $14.95

Index

NORMAN WILLOUGHBY

Management Consultant
specialising in project management

Technical Services

Management problems? How can I help? By either the rescue of a faltering project or assistance in the planning and documentation for new one.

Ninety percent of the time, the problems are simply those of planning and organisation. You will find it helps to bounce your ideas off a discerning veteran and may be pleasantly surprised at how many of the difficulties can be overcome by a few e-mail transmissions, a couple of phone calls, a fax or two and the submission of proposals, revised or completely new documents.

Plans of operation, organisation charts, schedules, procedures manuals and evaluations are meat and potatoes to me (or tofu and salad).

Small problems or large. There is no charge for a first opinion and reasonable rates - fixed price or hourly - thereafter.

I am prompt and reliable - and frank enough to tell you if I can't help you. Reading my books will give you an idea of how I work.

Call, fax or email.
Phone: 001 250-544-2094 Fax:: 001 250-544-1089
Email: normanw@primus.ca

View my web-page at:
http://home.primus.ca/-normanw

or request my one-page résumé